T0131596

Tracey, Don't Get Your New Coat Dirty

Memoirs of an Intuitive

by Tracey O'Mara

BALBOA.PRESS
A DIVISION OF HAY HOUSE

Balboa Press books may be ordered through booksellers or by contacting:

Balboa Press
A Division of Hay House
1663 Liberty Drive
Bloomington, IN 47403
www.balboapress.com
844-682-1282

Because of the dynamic nature of the Internet, any web addresses or
links contained in this book may have changed since publication and
may no longer be valid. The views expressed in this work are solely those
of the author and do not necessarily reflect the views of the publisher,
and the publisher hereby disclaims any responsibility for them.

The author of this book does not dispense medical advice or prescribe the use
of any technique as a form of treatment for physical, emotional, or medical
problems without the advice of a physician, either directly or indirectly. The
intent of the author is only to offer information of a general nature to help
you in your quest for emotional and spiritual well-being. In the event you use
any of the information in this book for yourself, which is your constitutional
right, the author and the publisher assume no responsibility for your actions.

Scripture quotations marked NIV are taken from THE HOLY BIBLE,
NEW INTERNATIONAL VERSION®, NIV® Copyright © 1973, 1978,
1984, 2011 by Biblica, Inc.® Used by permission. All rights reserved worldwide.

Print information available on the last page.

ISBN: 978-1-9822-7707-9 (sc)
ISBN: 978-1-9822-7709-3 (hc)
ISBN: 978-1-9822-7708-6 (e)

Library of Congress Control Number: 2021923696

Balboa Press rev. date: 12/15/2021

Dedication

This book is dedicated to my family on earth and in spirit, especially, Vic, Oliver, Lewis, Clair, Alex, and Mum.

Contents

Acknowledgments

I would like to acknowledge Vic, my soul mate, for all of his unwavering support, loving encouragement, positivity, and for always reminding me that laughter really is the best medicine; my beloved daughter-in-law, Victoria, for editing my writing and putting a sparkle on to my work; my loving sons, Oliver and Lewis, for proofreading and helping to edit, listening, supporting, and encouraging their crazy mum throughout; my dear Zoe, for bringing music to our lives and into my meditations; my grandsons, Ollie and Mateo, for thoughtfully waiting as I worked before showing me their newest projects; my dear friend, Barbara, for encouraging me and patiently listening to each emerging chapter and sharing her intuition, wisdom, and love along the way; Sherae, my soul sister, for all of her love, support, and gentle guidance and for boosting my confidence and helping me find the courage to write; and last but not least the legions of Angels, spirit guides, and benevolent beings of light working tirelessly beyond the veil to encourage us with their messages of inspiration, love, hope, joy and peace, always shining the light of Unconditional Love onto us while we navigate our way through the trials and tribulations of life.

A Letter from Ollie

"Dear Grandma,

How do the Angels do the amazing things they do? The reason I am asking is because I have been seeing them and I do not know why. One day, the Angel with blue wings gave me a Book of Knowledge. The book was about creatures, portals, and dimensions. How can the Angels have a book like this? Love, Ollie." (Age 8)

Dear Ollie,

Yes, the Angels do amazing things. I see them, too. The best that I can offer you is my own experience and to tell you the ways in which the Angels have helped me in my life. I hope that when you are older you will read this and that even if your questions are not all answered, you will know you are not alone in your experiences and that you are, in fact, divinely loved and protected.

I used to think that some things were impossible. Throughout my experience in life, I have come to realize that nothing is impossible, it is only that we have yet to experience it. Believe in the magic and the magic will appear.

Lots of Love, Grandma Tracey.

Preface

Why are we born?

Thrust into the school of hard knocks known as the third dimension, we incarnate into our wonderful earthly plane of duality. We forget everything we ever knew before birth and become totally dependent on the adults assigned to us. Their beliefs, their fears, and their experiences are draped upon our shoulders like invisible overcoats, fashioning and tailoring an artificial exterior over the true essence of our being that is better suited to their systems.

Do not be afraid to throw off the old overcoats to reveal your true essence. Shine the light of love into this dense reality to disperse negativity and clear and cleanse all past mistakes. In doing so, we will accomplish our shared goal of more enlightened states of being. The main mission of our souls is to reach enlightenment, that is, to transcend the stories created for and by us on earth to ascend into the most glorious light of God's love, thus illuminating His love into this plane of existence.

When we envision a person who has attained enlightenment, what do we see? Is it a monk sitting in meditation on a mountain top? Or do we see our imperfect selves facing life's challenges in the state of love, peace, and non-judgment?

Achieving enlightenment may sound like an enormous task for any of us to master. Is it even possible? I do believe the answer to be *yes*. The wisdom of the heart supersedes the mind. Once we are in tune with the heart, which is known as the moral compass, we are halfway there. We are all learning and growing on our own respective paths, no more or less, no better or brighter than one another. Having a spiritual gift does not indicate spiritual maturity or enlightenment. Each of us are bestowed with one gift or another, each and every one of us. What truly matters is how and why we use our gifts. Are we using our gifts for the greater good or to feed one's own ego? If the latter overrides the greater good, we have to ask the question: "Is this a misuse of our powers?"

At this time, we are tasked with sending light to each soul we encounter, activating the cellular gift of *remembrance*, helping to prepare and awaken the mind, body, and soul to a new, more loving way of being. I highly doubt it is possible to reach enlightenment when one's heart is not in the right place, whether or not one is considered to be a fantastic psychic, intuitive, healer or not. Only when the heart is open and filled with love, compassion, wisdom, and good intentions, is enlightenment attainable. As Paul said to the Corinthians: "If I have the gift of prophecy and can fathom all mysteries and all knowledge, and if I have a faith that can move mountains, but do not have love, I am nothing" (*New International Version,* Cor. 13.2).

The more your heart opens, the brighter your light becomes, attracting multitudes of benevolent beings of light to assist you on your quest to be light and to spread light. Once a more enlightened state of being is attained, no matter what chaos ensues on your path, your being will be filled with total peace, a deep understanding, and well-being. What a wonderful space to be in. Believe in yourself and never give up on your spiritual evolution.

Enlightenment is the very essence of truth. It is a deep knowing, understanding, and awareness of all that you are and all that is. It is an implicit trust in your soul's journey and the experiences you will encounter in your life in order to evolve. I chose everyone in my life and I am honored and blessed to have this wonderful adventure with them. This is my journey towards a more enlightened state of being. May it inspire you and ignite a sparkle of unconditional love, light, remembrance, and laughter within your own heart.

I was a shy, sensitive child, who did not want to be seen. For instance, upon hearing the song "Tracy," by the Cufflinks, playing on the radio, I would cringe and, even worse, if someone started singing it to me, I would feel deep discomfort from the embarrassment of being noticed. Not fully understanding why I felt everything so intensely, I found out in my adult years that I was a strong empath with the gifts of *clairvoyance*, the ability to see beyond the visible spectrum, combined with the gift of foresight; *clairaudience,* the ability to hear beings and information from another vibration, energy, or dimension; and *clairsentience,* similar to empathy, the ability to physically feel another's pain, emotions, or experience their thoughts. The difference between clairsentience and empathic ability is that those who are clairsentient are aware of the source of the feelings they experience, whereas the empath does not. For example, if an individual has sciatica, an empath will feel that pain in their own lower back, unaware it is just a transference of energy from the individual in pain. In the same situation, a clairsentient person will know that the sudden feeling of pain in their back is coming from another person who is experiencing sciatica, and that the individual they have come in contact with is the person suffering from it, without ever being told. Another example is that if an individual is going through a divorce or dealing with loss, a person with clairsentience will experience the same emotions of sadness, fear, hurt and anxiety, knowing that those feelings belong to someone else. An empath does not, thus these feelings from others can be mistaken for one's own feelings.

According to a recent exchange with an adept and accomplished astrologer, one who forecasts and assesses earthly events by observing and interpreting the locations of the stars and planets, my birth chart revealed that I was predestined to be spiritually and intuitively inclined. This astrologer was able to describe my personality and my essence down to the smallest detail. She described my heightened intuitive awareness, clairvoyance, sensitivities that others did not know about, and conflicts in my childhood regarding painful shyness, anxiety, and insecurity.

As a child, I felt everything to a heightened degree, not knowing why. When my awareness developed, I asked the Angels why I came to this life with so much sensitivity. They informed me that my soul wanted to learn emotional and mental strength. Part of my mission in this incarnation was to truly empathize and help others in the best way possible. I was also told I came with a small amount of my true energy because I wanted to see if I could overcome the temptations of shadow and reach a spiritual maturity by growing the light within, like a lotus flower that rises from the dirt and blossoms in the light, to enhance and fine tune the intuitive gifts bestowed onto me.

Our *soul contracts* are determined and agreed upon before leaving our true home of God's light of Unconditional Love and incarnating here on this earth. My understanding is that our eternal spirits learn and grow through our trials and tribulations on this earthly plane of duality (i.e., good and evil, light and dark, right and wrong). It is hard to believe that we would choose to be born into a tough life, enduring challenges through endless scenarios and possibilities. I believe some things in our contracts are set in stone and others are variable, depending on the choices life presents to us in moments in time. We live on a plane of free-will and choice. We choose our contracts, or life paths, with the help of wise elders in Spirit, creating the perfect plan for the lessons we would like to learn or overcome. Every miniscule detail is fine-tuned, right down to the exact moment of conception and birth. The very thought that the second you were born was prearranged and in accordance to your own astrological chart is mind blowing, to say the least; indicating the significance of divine timing. One of my many lessons was to learn patience. There was a time when I would regularly ask my guides when an event was going to occur. Their reply was: "when it is the right time".

To which I would respond, "when will it be the right time?"

Their reply would always be, "when it is divine time. Not Tracey's time." I eventually surrendered my expectations and learned to trust in divine timing, quickly realizing that everything happens exactly at the right moment in time. In all situations, I now ask: *what am I learning from this?* I might not like the situation or the answer, but I try to understand it and why it appeared on my life-path. When we are in spirit and situated in the light of Unconditional Love, it is easy to forget how hard life can be in the physical reality. In the grand scheme of things, human life is brief. We are here for only a moment in time, always returning to the light of Unconditional Love. I have seen many souls along the way and have total admiration for the ones who suffer so much strife and discord, yet remain filled with love, joy, and compassion: the ones living a life of positivity, regardless of their circumstance. They will certainly return home to the love of God with a badge of honor for completing the mission of their exceptionally difficult soul contracts. The biggest challenge some souls have is to stay on the path of light. Once a soul has fallen off of the path and steps into the shadow, they can become manipulative and abusive, wielding their power in a desire to harm others. This is a variable in their contract, or a possibility to fall into temptation which detours the individual from the path of light, one that the soul is aware of before incarnating. Are any of us supposed to do harm to others? No! We all have a choice of how we deal with our circumstances and whether or not to find the positive in a situation or to focus on the negative. We have the choice to become bitter and twisted, living in an incessant state of anger, spewing venom to all because of our own inner pain, insecurities, life experience, and frustrations. This only results in creating more challenges for the soul.

On the other hand, what some of us may perceive as a tough life is not necessarily so for the soul experiencing the life deemed "difficult". Furthermore, the ease or difficulty of one's life path does not determine its worth. All life is worthy and its value is intrinsic. Years and years ago, Vic, my husband, and Oliver, our son, and I had stopped off for a cup of tea and a snack at a small motorway cafe. With just two rows of tables and a narrow walkway between them, we situated ourselves diagonally to a mother and her young son, roughly around the age of eleven, whom many in the physical realm would consider to have Down syndrome. Shortly after we arrived, the mother and son got up to leave. As they walked by our table, the young boy stopped and placed his hand on top of mine which was resting on the table. I looked up and into the eyes of the old, majestic soul. He transmitted a radiant white light from his eyes that filled my heart and soul with the light of Unconditional Love and an unexplainable knowing. In that instant he blessed me. He smiled and nodded. I smiled and silently thanked him. He then lifted his hand from mine and continued on his journey. I turned to Vic and said, "you will never guess what just happened," and to my astonishment, Vic said, "he blessed you, didn't he?" In that exchange I had witnessed the most enlightened soul I have ever encountered, even to this day.

Tracey's Tricycle

MUM'S TENACIOUS ENERGY WAS ONE OF AN EXTROVERT: VIVACIOUS and rebellious; always the life and soul of the party. Her pretty face and petite frame, standing only four feet eleven inches, would have fooled you into thinking she was someone that could be walked over. Her stature never stopped her from standing up for her beliefs, especially in regards to the animal kingdom. Marion Butterworth adored dogs and would protect them at all cost. Speaking her mind was second nature to her, and her short fuse could lead to confrontations and explosive outbursts.

Once, as a small child, she called the RSPCA to report her landlord for abusing his Alsatians, which were chained up in the yard. He used to beat them with a belt buckle. Grandma Lily scolded Mum for placing the family in a situation which could have resulted in their eviction and subsequent homelessness. Mum was not in the slightest bit sorry. She had a love for animals that carried on throughout her life, always saying that she could trust an animal not to hurt her as humans often did.

Many years later, not long after dating my father, Roy, she fell pregnant with my brother, Lee. These two strong personalities were beguiled by each other, and trying to do the "right thing", they decided to make-a-go-of-it, marrying within twelve months of meeting.

My father came from the local town, which was a twenty-five-minute bus ride from Mum's village. Neither one of them drove, so I doubt they had much interaction during courtship before becoming pregnant and making this serious life choice.

They began married life living with his parents. Mum was twenty-four when she gave birth to Lee, during one of the coldest winters the UK had endured since 1659. It was known as "The Big Freeze", as even the sea froze inshore. Many infants did not survive that winter. Mum was grateful for my grandma and grandad and the perpetual warmth from the coal fire they maintained. Countless families were losing their youngest family members at this time. My grandma knew what it was to suffer the loss of a child. She had given birth to triplets and two died shortly after birth. Her third son died in the prime of his life. She was determined not to lose her grandson to the cold and succeeded in protecting him. My parents moved into a rented home just up the street from them soon after. I was born fourteen months after my brother, on the vernal equinox in 1964.

Mum described me as being a chubby-faced, mellow baby that just ate and slept, never complained, and just went with the flow. My brother on the other hand was quite a handful. Mum said he was born with an attitude. Perhaps he did not truly want to face the challenges that awaited him in his life.

The marriage of Roy and Marion went downhill at a rapid pace. Mum looked after us during the day and worked the night-shift to earn extra money. She enlisted the help of two teenage babysitters to care for us while my father continued his evening routine of visiting the local pub. Between her shifts at work, Mum still made sure to have my father's dinner ready and on the table for him when he arrived home from his job. One evening, Mum made him a rag pudding for dinner. Rag puddings are made with beef and onions wrapped in a suet pastry, tied in old strips of pillow cases, and simmered in a pan of boiling water. Funnily enough, they actually looked like little white pillowcases. Mum had made him this delicacy as a treat. She underestimated his arrival time from work and took the pudding out of the boiling water a little too early. The pudding had sat on the plate for a few minutes and lost its shine. When he walked in the kitchen and took one look at his dull rag pudding, he went into a fit of rage. His hand tightened into a hard fist, and before Mum could move,

Roy landed a punch to her left eye. By all accounts, Mum had a few black eyes in her time with my father.

While I do not have much mental recollection of their time together, the truth resided deep in my subconscious, forming a dislike for my father, no matter how kind he was to me. Although, I do remember when she left him because of a profound moment I experienced. It was one of my first soul-remembrances, shown to me by the Angels. *Soul-Remembrance* is the ability to see beyond the present reality and into the true essence of divine light.

In this instance, I was shown a glimpse of my soul contract signifying the end of a challenging time. We had fled from my father and had gone to stay at my maternal grandmother's house. I felt safe, secure, and loved there. A few months passed by swiftly. One day, Mum took me outside to play in the square situated at the front of Grandma Lily's cottage. The square consisted of a path surrounded by tall, nicely trimmed privet hedges. A well-maintained lawn was situated in the middle. Two skillfully carved wooden benches had been provided by a local carpenter for all the neighborhood to enjoy. Mum settled down on one of the delightful benches to read the daily newspaper, while I pedaled on my new blue tricycle. It was a gorgeous day and as my two-and-a-half-year-old little legs moved up and down with my feet pressed firmly on the pedals, a gentle warm breeze blowing in my face, I felt like I had ridden into a different realm. An iridescent golden sheen filled with love, radiant waves of peace, calm and happiness washed over my chubby little body. I heard my higher-soul-self distinctly say, "thank goodness that part of my life is over!" With this exclamation came a tremendous sense of relief, the weight of domestic violence was lifted off of my tiny shoulders. The incredible sense of peace and unconditional love I felt was a gift from the Divine, instigated by my Angelic Friends. While I did not have any understanding at the time of what had occurred, I have never forgotten this profound moment. It was forever etched in my memory giving me strength and hope for the journey ahead. I had *remembered*.

In hindsight, I believe I had written this moment into my life plan to give me a boost of energy and to be reminded of the light of God's Unconditional Love. How could I know and be aware of this as a toddler, otherwise?

Mum was an atheist and my family rarely shared any of their religious learnings, allowing me to find my own path without any pressure or expectation. I had an innate knowledge that there is a higher power, one that is so full of love, I would never be dissuaded to believe in anything else. We may call this loving presence the Great Spirit, God, the Almighty, Supreme Being, the Creator, a Higher Power, Mother-Father God, or Universal Love. Whatever our beliefs, we are dearly loved. The light of Unconditional Love is always present. We only need to remember to open our hearts and allow ourselves to receive.

I was given this inspiring message in my late twenties. My Angelic Friends advised me on how simple it is to live a more spiritual life. "Tracey," they said to me, "you must try and act with love and compassion for everyone and in everything you do." They explained, "you are then a conduit for divine light to flow through, planting light with every step you take. Thus, learning and growing spiritually every moment of every day regardless of what your mental mind thinks or your understanding of the metaphysical." I asked them their thoughts on religion. They explained that religion is a beautiful thing when the intentions and actions are based in love rather than power, control, and superiority. To help me understand, the Angels brought an image to my mind and I recalled an experience I shared with Lee in our childhood.

We were probably eight and nine years old at the time. Lee had thought it would be a good idea to go to the Sunday school his friends had raved about. Mum was not a church-goer, so we took the initiative to visit the local Methodist church on our own. I will never forget the feeling while being ushered by an adult to a small table in the far corner of the room, away from any of the other children. We were given crayons and a sheet of paper to color. An overwhelming sense that we did not belong filled my heart. I remember adults gathering at the front of the room, looking towards us while whispering their disdain. I was confused. From what my brother had said his friends told him about church, I thought we would be happy there. On one hand, it was being taught that Jesus loved and welcomed little children, and on the other, my brother and I were being made to feel out of place. It did not make sense to me.

Obviously, it was not Jesus who was running the Sunday school, and my brother and I were experiencing a prime example of spiritual snobbery as two little children who were rejected for not being quite what the community wanted us to be. I was so upset that I never went back and neither did Lee. Even though negative words were never spoken directly to us, the energy itself spoke volumes, as both thoughts and whispered words create energy, even if they are not heard by the subjects. The energy, or frequency, creates an atmosphere that can be felt.

Upon reflecting on this moment in my life as an adult and in more awareness, I was shown a scene from one of my past lives as another example. I closed my eyes, took a few deep breaths, and relaxed, honing in on the hazy image. As it began to clear, I saw my soul-self as a young Tibetan monk sitting in a circle with others in silent meditation. I had devoted my life to spiritual practice. I sensed a deep pride in my accomplishment. Although I had a beautiful feeling of achievement and I had done a marvelous job in that prior lifetime, one thing that I had not accomplished was the control of my ego. I could sense the feeling of self-righteousness emanating from my prior being. I was taken aback by this realization. How could I have been so unaware? The Angels advised me that my stubborn pride had not allowed me to believe that there could be another path to enlightenment. In that life, I thought I had attained all of my spiritual goals. I knew in an instant how wrong this beautiful young man before me was. His naivety in God's spiritual law was not uncommon, we are all learning and growing. The Angels moved to a clip in the future of this incarnation. Not long after the first memory the Angels had shown me of the life of this monk, I was shown another memory of his monastery being invaded. The young monk was forced to escape. While walking over the mountains and learning the lesson of humbleness, he gathered knowledge from the many travelers he encountered. One traveler in particular, a yogi, became a lifelong friend and teacher. In observing the many wonderful souls he had encountered, he realized there were many paths to enlightenment, not just his way. It took the young man a long time to forgive himself for his ego, which was another invaluable lesson for him: *forgive oneself, forgive all.*

Come from your heart, dear Reader, regardless of your beliefs or background. If our actions are filled with good intentions, and our hearts are shining the Creator's light into the world, then wrong doings and misuse of power do not exist. In this way, each soul simply does their best to gather knowledge and truth in the light of oneness.

I still come across spiritual snobbery to this day. The energy that is given out, that I can physically feel, is the attitude that says, "our club is better than yours". Perhaps this is due to the cellular memory from my Sunday school experience, which taught me to instantly recognize this energy. I might add that it does not trigger anger, sadness, or feelings of inadequacy within me, as I made peace with it a long time ago. We have to remind ourselves: there is not better or worse, there are many paths to God. Isn't the key just to be on the path?

The Creator loves us all. God would never differentiate between any of his children. He wants us to grow spiritually, bringing light into our hearts, thus, overcoming the distortion of this earthly plane created by the collective misuse of freewill.

We can transmute negative energy into light, creating more of the feeling of having heaven on earth.

My daughter-in-law, Victoria, wrote a beautiful pondering on how she envisions God:

I suppose to most everyone the afterlife is an enigma. The religious hold laws about the afterlife, such as, the virtuous and upright will find themselves in an eternal paradise, Heaven, Janna, The Elysian Fields, Nirvana, etc. and the wicked will be condemned to either a place of eternal pain or will revisit life on earth in cycles of reincarnation until freed from karmic actions or enlightenment. Images of a grandfatherly figure with a gloriously soft, curly white beard with opalescent eyes that hold the entire universe, filled with kindness and love and the knowledge of every thought and every action committed, come to mind. Angels gather to either side, holding the scales of each person's rights and wrongs. Perhaps the afterlife is a celestial garden high above the earth resting on interstellar clouds made of thick gypsophila and hydrangea from a spectrum of starlight hidden to our eyes, as such beauty is only for the worthy. But to this grandfatherly figure, the scales matter not so much, as he already knows the hearts of every creature in existence.

Expectations of what the afterlife entails are as varied and as personal as fingerprints. The question of what has happened to a loved one now that he or she is lost on the earthly plane is answered more accurately by the consoling (or not so consoling) fantasies of the heart, than any science currently available. The truth is that while we are alive and breathing, there is only the collective imagination of our species as a basis for any theory developed about the afterlife. And there is not much that can be done about that reality.

I loved Victoria's musing on the Creator. Her sentence, "opalescent eyes that hold the entire universe filled with kindness and love," this is the Creator I know and love. Why would our all-loving Father-God bring his wrath onto His children, whom He loves unconditionally? He may be disappointed in our behavior and speak the truth through the wisdom of His Heart, giving us guidance through His helpers, the Angels, and countless benevolent beings of light assigned to His children on earth, gently whispering into our ears from beyond the veil to get back onto the right path.

Can you imagine ceasing to love your own child or grandchild when they have been naughty? Although we have to show them the difference between right and wrong, most of us never doubt our love for them, even when correcting behavioral issues. In my own experience, I have had nothing but encouragement and love, no judgement or criticism from the Angels. Trust me when I say I have needed and had plenty of guidance from a higher power. Perhaps it was always there just to keep me on track and to remind me of my purpose in life. There are so many conflicting energies on the earth plane, we can easily find ourselves slipping or falling off of our mission of light. Yet, it is never too late to change. We all have to be responsible for our actions. Acknowledge them, forgive them, and do not repeat our prior mistakes.

Not many souls exist who are inherently evil, even though there are hearts that seem to be devoid of goodness, empathy, compassion, and love; hearts that never take responsibility for their heinous crimes against others, a tiny glimmer of light must still shine within. As mentioned, the earthly plane is one of duality. Where there is light, there is shadow. In these dark hearts, the shadow is so strong it is almost impossible for the light to grow. These souls keep reincarnating until they choose to open their hearts to the all-loving Angels waiting patiently to show them the way to redemption and God's loving embrace. I asked the Angels why there is such a reluctance from some souls to go to the light? Some souls are fearful of their soul review. The Angels reminded me nothing ever goes unnoticed, each and every soul is responsible for their actions. When we have good intentions, we are recognized for them, even if things worked out in a less than ideal way. If we have bad intentions, we only end up hurting others and ourselves, and that hurt follows us. Each and every soul who goes to the light has a soul review. While being held in the light of unconditional love without judgement, every action good, bad, and indifferent is played out before us like a movie screen except we simultaneously experience and feel the depth of emotions we created for ourselves and others, even down to feelings of the family members and loved ones affected by our actions; like a chain reaction of emotions. There are always consequences to our actions and many souls spend lifetimes making up for prior misdeeds. Some souls are aware of the pain they have caused others and so they are reluctant to atone for their actions. However, the earth plane is one of duality and a very small number of souls, such as dark hearts, like the power this realm affords them. Regardless of what they do, the light will always prevail in the end.

I believe Father-God is the source of creation and is all-knowing, loving, and wise, immeasurable for our level of intelligence to begin to fathom. How can there be so much division and strife in this third dimensional world when we share a benevolent Higher Power? The true essence of love is freedom. Each and every soul is afforded freewill and free choice which is bestowed on us by Father-God in the hope that we live our lives in the knowledge that we have a moral responsibility to choose the path of light. However, not every soul chooses light in every instance. There is so much division in our world at present that The Angels want to remind us not to get caught up in the shadow's agenda of division. Each soul is born into this third dimensional reality with the God given right to choose light or dark. Each soul has a higher self that knows what is right or wrong for them at that moment in time depending on a certain belief system or indoctrination. This can change at any moment, which again emphasizes the right to choose freely. One might not understand, like or agree with the opinions or choices of others. The key is to stay neutral, as the Higher Power does, about the beliefs and opinions of others and not allow yourself to be drawn into the shadow's agenda of the division of humanity. Once we stay in our own lane, we join with the energy of unification for humanity which we can all agree is very much needed in our conflicted world. This does not mean to silence one's voice. We all have the free will and free choice to express our opinions, to stand up for what is believed to be right, without forcefully imposing one's beliefs on another. When one stays energetically neutral, another is more likely to take what resonates within their heart center and add it to their own truth, awakening to different ideas and possibilities. The Angels also say when a soul's intentions are truly good, they will not bring harm to another. In other words, we have a moral responsibility to choose well. The act of staying neutral about the beliefs helps to achieve one's own inner peace and to help release the ego's desire to control others through will and force. In order for our beliefs to be honored, we honor the right for others to believe otherwise. It is only in this way can we truly love our neighbors.

I also believe there must be a balance between male and female. God made us in his image, or as Genesis of the Bible states: "And God said, let us make man in our image, in our likeness" *(New International Version,* Genesis 1:26*)*. I have always sensed the existence of the divine feminine. The Blessed Mother, a counterpart to the Creator. A perfect balance of male and female. The female counterpart of the Creator has been known in many cultures throughout time. The ancient Romans knew her as Terra Mater, and Greeks referred to her as Gaia, both meaning Earth Mother. Traces left in the Book of Kings suggest the Hebrew God, Yahweh, had a female counterpart, named Asherah. In all instances She was revered as the Divine's wife. She is all nurturing, loving and harmonizing, presiding over the earth, helping us to balance our emotions, creating miracles bestowed on us through our divine right to receive as part of God's perfect plan. Omnipresent, their essence lies like a spark of light within our hearts, waiting for us to awaken and ignite the light of Unconditional Love we are all gifted with. Once ignited, it is impossible to do anything that feels morally wrong. In turn, one's light becomes brighter and brighter, radiating out like a beautiful thread, merging with the threads of others, eventually infiltrating every dark corner of the world, and blessing all with a powerful new way of being; finally bringing love, compassion, forgiveness and peace.

This should instill you with a sense of pride knowing your purpose here is to bring and share the light of God's Love.

Grandma's Safe Haven

GRANDMA LILY'S LITTLE COTTAGE RESIDED IN A GROUP OF VILLAGES, called Saddleworth, in Northern England, which is tucked neatly in a valley between green hills and trees, alongside moors, fields, and meadows. The cottage was quaint, with just one front door entrance, a small living area, a tiny kitchen and two bedrooms. Some of my fondest memories are of sitting around the coal fire, rolling sheets of newspaper into sticks, and tying them into knots in preparation to light the fire. The aroma created by the fire lighters is one I still enjoy. This aromatic memory was not about the smell, but the sense of love, security, and peace I felt while with my grandma. Grandma Lily was my Mum's mum. She was always calm and never raised her voice. She used to listen to the tracks from "The Sound of Music" on her old record player, while making paper flowers and little silk bags filled with lavender buds that were tied with different colored ribbons. The song, "My Favorite Things," must have inspired her to tap into the pot of creative energy. The movie, "The Sound of Music", which was based on a true story, was released in March, 1965. The film was a huge success, becoming the highest grossing film of all time. Our whole family loved it. Perhaps it was such a huge hit because so many had gone through terrible times just twenty years earlier, during World War II. This story, with its message of triumph over adversity, gave a sense of relief and served as a reminder of how important our freedom and peace are.

My Grandma had been widowed at the age of forty-nine. Grandad had fought in World War II and after the war ended in 1945, he was released from the military. Within a year, his health declined. After falling numerous times for no apparent reason, he was diagnosed with a debilitating neurological disease, disseminated sclerosis. This slowly robbed him of his mobility and speech. Mum recalled her father being bedridden on a small cot in the living room of their tiny home for almost ten years before he passed away at fifty years of age. Grandma, with two children to raise, had selflessly and solely nursed him for all of that time. Life's knocks had certainly toughened her up. She lost her twin sister, Lucy, at the age of thirteen, and a baby brother, yet kept her heart open to loving others, despite knowing the feeling of loss. To overcome her grief, she channeled her energy instead into serving those she loved. I am glad to have even a modicum of her courageous and strong cellular memory running through my veins.

My grandad's illness had a significant impact on Mum, who was only nine years old when he fell ill. She recalls hearing him wail in distress almost every day. Money was tight, and although Mum had holes in her shoes and patched up clothes, she ignored the endless tormenting from her peers and studied hard to pass the Eleven Plus exam, which would allow her to attend grammar school. She was proud of this achievement. Her dream was to become an English teacher. This was until her mother dropped the bombshell that due to the change in circumstances, her father's illness, she would not be able to attend grammar school. They did not have enough money for the bus fare. Mum's friend had also passed the exam and she had hoped her friend's mother would allow her to catch a ride with them to and from the grammar school. This would have solved the dilemma, but her heart sank on the realization that her friend was not going to offer her a ride, and she gloomily accepted her fate.

Grandma never remarried or even dated anyone to my knowledge. Her love for my grandad must have been so strong. An experience that I had with my grandma in my teen years helped me to fully understand their bond. I had been having some teenage ups and downs and popped around to Grandma's house for some peace of mind and encouragement. Grandma was on her way out, explaining to me that she was going to her niece's house to see a woman. Luckily, she invited me along. Off we went to the bus stop. The bright orange double decker bus came to a screeching halt alongside us. After promptly boarding, we took our seats at the front for the thirty-minute ride. This was quite an outing for my grandma; she did not like to go out on her own after dark.

The whole adventure intrigued me. Who was this lady? Why was Grandma so excited to see her? Eventually, the bus pulled into our stop and from there it was a ten-minute walk to our relative's home. The dark cool night air breeze left a chill on my ears and the tip of my nose. I could feel the anticipation growing with every step. I knew in my heart something special was about to happen, but had no clue as to what. We had arrived. Grandma rang the bell and the door swung open. We eagerly stepped into the living room. Sat on the couch was a little old lady with silver hair and deeply penetrating steel-gray eyes. She looked over to me and smiled. I felt an instant warmth in my heart.

After a polite exchange, Jean ushered me into the kitchen as she whispered in my ear, "Grandma and the lady need time on their own to chat." She said, "she has a special gift. She talks to deceased loved ones and the Angels."

Wow, I thought to myself, *this is incredible.* A small amount of time passed when suddenly I began to feel sick. My menstrual cycle was about to start and every now and again I would get the most excruciating cramps that would make me vomit. Jean did not know what to do. I tried to reassure her that I did not have food poisoning and there was nothing that would alleviate the pain. We had previously tried all of the over-the-counter medication to no avail. I had to wait it out. After hearing the commotion, Grandma called us to the living room. The elderly lady beckoned me to sit next to her on the couch. All were very concerned at my discomfort and pasty pallor. The elderly lady gently touched my arm as she asked me how long I had been suffering from these attacks. The words, "ever since my menstrual cycle started," had barely escaped my mouth, when I felt this overwhelming warmth enveloping every cell of my being and the pain instantly subsided. I exclaimed, "the pain has just vanished!"

The elderly lady looked into my eyes and said, "it will do, love, I am also an energy healer." She reassured me that my problem would soon disappear completely and a few months later it did. I was astounded. I thought to myself: *what a beautiful gift. I would love to be able to help people in that way.* I never in my wildest dreams thought that my life would take me on a similar path.

On the way home, Grandma opened up about her experiences with the afterlife. She shared with me that she had always felt Grandad's presence, he had guided her often, and she would even feel his gentle loving touch on her shoulder. It was incredible to witness a love that had outlasted death. Grandma shared that she had been a spiritualist for many years, regularly attending her small local church in Uppermill, Saddleworth, where mediums, clairvoyants, energy healers, and believers in the afterlife congregated and shared their gifts. This was the first time she had ever shared her spiritual inclinations with me.

On hearing this I was taken back to a mysterious childhood memory, which Grandma later clarified for me. Some crisis had occurred and Mum had needed to drop us off with Grandma, who was at this small building. We entered the foyer. It was all very hush-hush. We were forbidden to enter the main room. We were made to sit quietly until Grandma came out, and she was not at all pleased with Mum. Children were not allowed at these gatherings. Lee and I waited on a little wooden bench, trying not to move. Soon, childhood curiosity got the better of us. We snuck quietly off the bench and made our way toward the entrance of the main room. Lee gently pushed the door open, just a crack, so we could peek in. Simultaneously, the congregation got up to exit. My Grandma spotted us peeping through the door and ran to us. She hurriedly ushered us out. We heard amongst the excited chatter of the crowd the mention of ancient Egypt and a Pharaoh's mask. This was double-Dutch to two small children from the English working class. The memory struck me with a sudden recognition. I still get a warm feeling in my heart when I see that spiritualist church from my mysterious childhood memory.

I found these new revelations that Grandma Lily shared to be incredible. I went home that evening with more reassurance and hope than ever before. My own paranormal encounters started to hold some meaning.

Many years later, while in Sedona, Arizona, while I was training to be a past life regression therapist, I was able to make a connection with the feelings of recognition I experienced as a child when first hearing about Egypt and my soul's journey. I was regressed back into the life of a fourteen-year-old Egyptian servant girl. Although I did not have any recollection of my name, I knew I was not able to verbalize due to having the tip of my tongue removed. I was a feisty, chatty child and this had irritated my previous master. He was emotionally unstable and prone to violent outbursts. Hence, the extreme punishment of cutting the tip of my tongue off. Not being able to speak, I listened well and learned the healing art of administering herbs and aromatic oils. My new master had many skin problems and the thought that he might smell bad as a result antagonized him. He associated uncleanliness with impurity, and smelling good indicated a sacred presence. I felt privileged to have this important job and my second master was kind to me. He liked the gentle touch of my hands as I used the oils to soothe his painful legs. I was also trusted to collect the aromatic oils from the priests. My master held a prominent position in the community which made this possible. This gave me a sense of pride and a small amount of freedom. I was enjoying life when suddenly my master passed away. This came as quite a shock.

I helped to embalm his body while preparations were made in his tomb. Jars were filled with different kinds of food, bread, jewels, and ornaments and everything my master needed for the afterlife. When finished, three of us had been chosen to go to the afterlife with him. I recalled receiving a fatal blow to the back of my head. Still in a semiconscious state when the tomb was closed, the sense of fear of being trapped in this small dark place was absolutely terrifying, as I was entombed alive.

This glimpse into the past helped me understand a few fears I had carried throughout my younger years and well into my thirties. One of them was fear of the dark. I could never settle down for the night unless the landing light was turned on in the house. I also felt extremely uncomfortable in confined spaces. I greatly enjoy essential oils and have studied aromatherapy, never realizing why the smell of frankincense would nauseate me and cause my heart to pound, no matter how much I appreciated its therapeutic qualities. The ancient Egyptians used frankincense in burial rituals as an embalming substance, aiding in covering up the smell of the dead body. The cellular memory from this lifetime was being triggered by the smell of frankincense, the memory of being in the dark and being trapped to death. After this revelation, I lost my fear of the dark and of confined spaces. While I still feel a little queasy on smelling frankincense, it is nothing quite as bad as it used to be. The cellular memory engrained so deeply began to heal after my past life regression.

Father

My father, Roy, was a short man with straight, mousy-brown hair and green eyes. I do not have any pictures of him. Perhaps Mum threw them all away. I never doubted that he loved us in his own way. I only felt that he spent far too much time playing the victim rather than realizing he had created his own reality and his life was the consequence of his actions.

My father had moved back in with his parents after the divorce. I sensed they all had resentment towards Mum for leaving him. Mum told me that my grandma always turned a blind-eye to my father's abusive behavior, while on the other hand, my grandad always intervened and stood up for her. At least she had one ally in my father's family. In my adult years, Mum told me of another incident that occurred after she had left him. He tracked her down to a local restaurant, walked over to the table where she was sitting, and knocked her off her chair with one swipe of his hand to the side of her head. Mum's two male friends stepped in and manhandled him out of the building. They were all appalled at my father's treatment of her.

I always admired Mum's stance regarding my father's place in our lives. While she boldly stood up to his abuse and had the courage to leave him, she did not use Lee and I against him. During my childhood, she never once mentioned a word about it to us children. I knew that she did not like my father, but she never complained about him or brought us into their issues.

I did not spend much time with our father after she divorced him. Perhaps it was that final assault that put an end to our regular contact with him. My brother and I used to visit one day a year, on the 26th of December, which was also the only time we saw our grandparents. I did feel a great love for them and enjoyed our time together, contrary to how I felt towards my father. On the one day a year we visited, he used to take us to his parent's house and then pop to the pub, spend a few hours there, and come back, have dinner and make small talk, then take us home. He was never mean to us. It was the tone of his voice when quizzing us on Mum or our home life, which spoke volumes. He would fish for information he could use against her. It amazes me when I look back how I could sense this at a very young age and my stubborn character would never engage in his self-pity and dirt-digging.

I found out many years later from a family friend that Lee and I used to try to pull him off of Mum while he was beating her. That is probably why I never took to liking him— that and the fact he was really a stranger to me. I stopped going to see my father when I turned twelve years old. He had made a comment to my brother and I, chastising us for not bringing Christmas gifts for our grandparents. How could we have brought Christmas gifts when Mum did not have any money to spare? I can remember feeling upset and anxious and could not wait to go home.

My next contact with my father was not until six years later. His mother was turning eighty years old and Lee and I had been invited to the party. I did not want to go, which was typical of me at the time, not wanting to face my fears. Mum and my stepfather, Peter, encouraged me to go. I went and had an enjoyable time, and then retreated back into my previous way of life. This can seem quite cold to many who have had loving relationships with their fathers. I questioned myself endlessly and felt guilty. Lee, on the other hand, found a way to maintain a loving relationship with him.

Life moved forward and our meetings continued to be sporadic. When my father was in his early fifties, he had a mild stroke and I was called to the hospital. This should have been a time of connection. Sadly, it was not. As we sat at his hospital bedside, he started spewing venom about Mum, again. After all these years, he was still creating his own misery. I could not stay long listening to his nonsense. Once again, his actions had unwittingly pushed me away. I had already worked through my feelings and stopped resenting him long before, and at this point, I felt only pity. What a sorry state he had created for himself, one of anger and bitterness for over twenty years. I stopped contact with him until by fate we ended up living in the same neighborhood.

I am ashamed to say, I used to hide if I saw him coming. This was my continued "ostrich" energy, burying my head in the sand. I hid until I had gathered enough emotional strength and eventually told myself I was going to face this issue head on, sincerely trying to connect with him. So that is exactly what I did. I was around the age of thirty at the time. With encouragement from my husband, Vic, my father and I began meeting up from time to time until he sank back into old patterns and started playing the victim again. I once again detached from him without his resistance. Apparently, his philosophy towards his children was: "they know where I am if they want me." He was true to his word. Unfortunately for him, he had not taken the initiative to build a good relationship with me, and therefore, I never wanted, needed, or expected anything from him. I could never understand why he would go to the bar for a few hours on the only day of the year we visited. I had worked through many of my emotions regarding my father, but this had left me with some residual anger until my Angelic Friends showed me a different perspective. They asked me to consider that perhaps he felt it too painful to see his children, knowing that he had missed out on seeing them grow over the years. Or, possibly that he did not know what to do or say as the relationship was not given the care it needed to develop. He may have felt intense guilt for this. It may have also been that he could not release his anger towards Mum and found it too difficult to hide, which could have exacerbated his desire to drink.

With the help of my Angelic Friends, I came to the conclusion it was all of the above. I gained a great amount of peace within my heart with this realization. Life became busy but continued to move along nicely. I soon became pregnant with my second child. I was only a few months along in my pregnancy when I received a crystal-clear message from the Angels: "Tracey, your father isn't going to be on the earth for much longer. If you would like to reconnect, it would be a good time. Be aware, your father will pass not long after your child is born." I took the time to mull over this message. I relayed this information to Vic, who wondered as much as I did what my course of action would be. I decided to push the idea to some small corner of my mind.

The months passed and my belly grew larger and larger. I was told by the Angels that my child would be born two weeks earlier than my due date. Two weeks to the day I was due, Vic, Oliver, and I were walking around our local shopping mall, picking out new carpets for our living room. When we stopped for dinner, Vic teased me, asking, "what had happened to the baby coming two weeks early?" as the message I received had plainly stated.

We laughed and I said, "maybe I got it wrong."

Two hours later, we were on the couch watching Jeremy Beadle's: "You've Been Framed" on television. Between fits of lighthearted giggles and belly-laughs at home videos of puppies attacking hand puppets and babies splashing each other in paddling pools, I felt a gush and said, "Vic, my waters broke."

"Not now, Jeremy Beadle's on," Vic joked.

Vic took me to the hospital. I informed everyone that the baby would be born before the day was done. They all laughed and said that I had not even started labour. This was true, labour had not started, but I knew that I was going to deliver within the next hour. Just around 10:00 PM, intense labour pains began. I asked Vic to fetch the midwife, who was arranging to move me out of delivery and into a room on the ward to wait. He had the flu at the time and felt terrible. Still not believing that our baby would be born any time soon, he exited the delivery room at a slow shuffle to find her. Minutes later, the midwife arrived to check on me and discovered I had fully dilated. All of a sudden it was pandemonium, with yells of, "the baby is coming!"

Lewis was born at 10:53 PM. There had not even been enough time to receive medication for pain relief, unless you count Vic having a cup of cold medicine to ease his flu symptoms.

Although I had an easy birth, I suffered from postnatal depression. The health visitor and doctor came to visit me at home, offering medication, which I promptly refused. As the tears streamed down my face, I assured everyone that I knew what it was that was ailing me, and whatever I was to go through, I was strong enough to get through it all. I was blessed to have had an understanding doctor and health visitor. Coincidentally, my health visitor was also a client of mine and she trusted my judgment.

Vic would phone me constantly throughout his work days out of concern. My emotional behavior was entirely out of character. I was unable to leave the house on my own except to drop off Oliver at school and pick him up, again. I bawled uncontrollably all the way home each time after dropping him off. This continued for some time. A few weeks passed when I received a message from Mum to say my father had been diagnosed with terminal lung cancer. She then asked if I was going to go and see him. I was at a loss for what to say. I had not even been able to leave the house, how could I have faced this? I told her that I did not feel I had the strength to see him.

A few more weeks passed and I slowly began to improve, venturing back out into the world, and in what felt like no time at all, a few months had passed. I happened to be driving passed the bottom of the street where my father's house was situated, when I heard an unmistakable message from my spirit guides: "Tracey, this is the last day your father will be on the earth. If you want to see him, you should go now. If not, you must live with your choice." I thanked my Angelic Friends for giving me this message. I had a choice. I chose not to go.

That evening, I received a phone call with the message that my father had died. Vic and Oliver, who were still concerned for my emotional wellbeing, asked how I was coping. It was such a strange feeling; I had an overwhelming sense that a chapter of my life had closed. Two days later, my father's spirit came to me asking if I would forgive him of any wrongdoings which had affected our ability to develop a relationship while in the physical. Immediately upon feeling the love and sincerity he had in spirit, I forgave him. I then reflected on my time as an adult and my own role in our relationship, the opportunities I might have also missed to heal and grow, and asked the same forgiveness from him. I also asked him to forgive himself and told him that I would work on forgiving myself.

I did not attend his funeral. Why would I play the grieving daughter after his death, when I could not see him in life? I have been asked many times if I had made the right choice. In that moment in time: yes; overall: maybe, maybe not. At the time, I felt that I should have had the courage to face my fears rather than always trying to hide from them. This was a huge challenge for me and my father was the person who brought the lesson to the forefront. If I could face and forgive him for his transgressions, I could face and forgive anyone. On the other hand, I was suffering from postnatal depression. I did not feel I had the emotional strength or courage to face him and perhaps he was not ready, either. But Roy was not alone through his illness and passing. Lee did what I could not, assisting and being present for our father in his time of need. Throughout our father's illness, Lee visited him, listened to him, and cared for him in ways that might seem simple, like offering to shave the stubble off of our father's face for him, but were actually intimate and meaningful moments for both of them.

On reflection, it was all divine perfection. This lesson has helped me when counseling others in similar situations. It was almost impossible to have absolute forgiveness while he was alive.

What could not take place in life always takes place in death when our souls are ready. My father, surrounded by Angels and standing in the light of Unconditional Love, made the journey back to this realm open-hearted, so that final healing between us could take place.

I feel honored and blessed to have witnessed this remarkable deep healing happen to others, numerous times. Once the burden of guilt is lifted through forgiveness, especially while one or both souls are still incarnate on the earth, a powerful and positive gift for all humanity ensues. Thus, healing the cellular memory of our ancestral line, preventing a transference of negative emotions onto future generations.

The Angels always tell me that forgiveness is extremely important for the spiritual evolution of humanity. They say: "We all know when we have done wrong. It does not feel right in our heart center." The heart is our moral compass. The mind always tries to justify our poor decisions or actions, ignoring the call from the heart. Once we are brave enough to pay attention to that little niggle, we realize we were wrong; we then begin to listen to the wisdom of the heart, which is not always easy because feelings of intense guilt may begin to overwhelm us. The key is to forgive yourself. In doing so, you learn to forgive all.

I will never forget a profound teaching I had on truth and forgiveness. This experience occurred in my late teens. I had an angry exchange with my mum. I cannot even remember what had started the argument. Home life could be difficult, occasionally, and, like many teens, I was behaving a little selfishly. Mum had a sharp tongue and in the middle of the argument, she yelled, "I should have put you and your brother in a children's home when I had the chance!"

The emotional dagger pierced my heart so deeply it felt physical. Then the anger rushed through me and I am ashamed to say: I retorted back, "well you should have done, we might have been better off!"

I marched upstairs, slammed my bedroom door, and locked myself in my room. Feelings of anger and sadness filled my mind and heart. Absorbed in my own self-pity, I started to feel the loving and calming presence of my Angelic Friends. I telepathically said, "Dear God, I am sorry for my poor behavior."

The Angel's reply was not what I was expecting. The Angel said, "Are you really sorry, Tracey, or do you just think you should say that you are sorry because you think we want to hear you say it?" I thought about this for a moment. I was still angry. On feeling my truth, I knew I was not sincerely sorry. I said to the Angels that I was not sorry at all.

"Yes, we know Tracey," they said, "because it did not come from your heart center. If it does not come from your heart, it is not worth the breath you have used to speak the words. It is ok to be angry and frustrated. Allow yourself time to process the situation, forgive your mum, and forgive yourself."

A few weeks later, after a few more ups and downs, I had managed to process everything. On reflection, I was truly sorry for my part in this barrage of emotional wounding. Mum and I had long since made up and things had started to settle down at home. I now sensed it was time to check back in with my Angelic Friends. "I am really sorry for my prior poor behavior," I told them.

"Yes, we know, Tracey, because it came straight from your love-filled heart center."

The expectation of me to apologize was not placed there by God or the Angels. It is just something I used to do, probably to address my own guilt when sensing I might have done or said something that was not considered godly. The message was so profound and full of love, I have spent my life trying to speak with loving truth from the wisdom of my heart. If my feelings are anything but heart centered, I try to stay neutral, knowing that was okay. This philosophy on life can be difficult in instances when one feels their buttons are being pushed, but once mastered, life becomes more peaceful and a lot less complicated.

While my father and I had our reconciliation after his passing, I have also been blessed to have witnessed reconciliations between loved ones brought about by those in spirit while both parties were still here in the physical. On one such occasion, Vic, the children, and I were visiting with Vic's parents, Ettie and Ernie. We had eaten a lovely Sunday dinner and, after washing the dishes, we sat down to chat while the children played. I usually was not disturbed by the spirit world while spending time with my family. This day was an exception. Ettie sat in a cozy one seated chair placed against the living room wall. All of a sudden, she felt the hands of an invisible soul touch her head and gently brush her hair. Quite startled and a little alarmed, she exclaimed: "who's that?"

I sensed it was the spirit of her deceased mother, Alice, whom I had never met. Alice had come on the wings of love to deliver an important message to her daughter. I clearly heard Alice say, "your sister, Beryl, isn't very well." Ettie and Beryl had been estranged over some small argument for nearly a year. They loved each other tremendously and being alienated from one another had been tough on them. Vic and I could see the message stirred a lot of confusion within Ettie.

Shortly after, we gathered up the children and said our goodbyes. On our way home, I relayed to Vic that I had sensed his auntie Beryl was not going to be in the physical for long and his grandma had come through to help his mum and aunt make their peace. Ettie, having reflected on the message I passed on to her from her mother, phoned her brother, Victor, to ask if he knew anything about Beryl's health. He did and let Ettie know that she had a few issues, but nothing serious. This eased her troubled mind.

The days following that exchange passed by the same way they usually did with school and work. We always looked forward to the end of the week and taking the children to see their grandparents. It was not long before Sunday was upon us again and we were visiting Ettie and Ernie's home to share a meal, chat, and enjoy time with each other. During a lengthy conversation, Ettie revealed that she had just received news that morning that Beryl had been admitted to hospital. As soon as this was brought up, Ettie's double clasp wristwatch was suddenly undone by invisible hands and fell off. The spirit of Alice was once again trying to get our attention. I said, "your mum's here again and she's nudging you to think about Beryl." Ettie nervously said that she was unsure of what to do, as her brother said Beryl was fine.

Alice's words came loud and clear into my mind: "I'm advising you to go and see Beryl. It's a good time to make your peace."

Ettie thought it through and decided to visit her sister. The trivialities of the past soon dissipated and once again, two sisters were united in love. A few weeks later, Beryl made her transition to the spirit world.

I had not realized at that moment the significance of Alice undoing Ettie's watch. While reflecting back on this, it dawned on me that she could not have been any more specific with her message: it was TIME.

We have a finite amount of time during our experiences here on earth. While healing and forgiveness does take place in the spiritual realm and in the loving embrace of God's Unconditional Love, the best use of our time is to forgive and love one another while we are still physically present on earth and make the most of it together. If we can learn to forgive the soul of another, even while we cannot necessarily forgive their actions, we can find peace in our own hearts in this physical reality, making us receptive to more peace and joy in our lives.

Decades later, while we had already been living in California for some years, Ettie asked me if I would buy her a night-and-day clock, which I promptly did and I had it shipped directly to her home in Mossley, England. I did not think anything of it at the time, however random the request might have seemed, and was just happy to have been able to do something nice for her.

Meanwhile, our youngest child, Lewis, now grown, had enlisted in the U.S. Army and we were preparing for him to leave for bootcamp, and Kaya, our oldest granddaughter, was visiting us from England. As a result, we had packed in many short trips around Southern California to entertain the both of them and spend time together as a family. The days passed quickly. A few weeks later, Ettie unexpectedly made her transition, accepting the hand of her loving husband, Ernest, and joining him in spirit. In retrospect, I believe Alice once again was trying to pass an indirect message to me, one that I might recognize as meaning that time-was-of-the-essence, in order to alert us of Ettie's transition.

Police Intervention

Much of the fear and anxiety I experienced as an adult developed in my early years, even from memories I had suppressed, or events which had happened when I was too young to understand them. However, the same can be said about the light I witnessed in others before knowing what that light meant. The short stay with Grandma Lily after Mum left my father came to an end when Mum had found someone new. We left Grandma's house and moved into a small abode in the neighboring village. The two-bedroom row cottage was situated on a steep hill, backing onto farmland. The small area was commonly known as "Bunkers". I loved life in this little cottage with Mum, Lee, some furry little friends from the fields, and a vague recollection of a nice man that used to tell us stories about monkeys. I thought this man was a figment of my childhood imagination until Mum confided in me in recent years that there was a man, we now call him the invisible man, who moved in with us for less than a year. Allegedly, he was one of the police officers who dealt with the harrowing case of The Moors murders. He had left his family to be with Mum, but could no longer cope with the guilt and scandal and went back to them. In hindsight, he had just witnessed recordings of a small child being tortured and murdered. It was no wonder he had guilt for leaving his own family. Even though my memory of him was vague, I recall him being kind to us.

That feeling of niceness did not happen as much as you would have expected a small child to experience. The era I was born into was the Swinging Sixties: a time of social change. The function of divorce was adapting to new concepts; sexual liberation became popular due to the introduction of the contraceptive pill; and women were receiving fairer pay and more equal rights in the workplace. Mum embraced this new way of life, especially after the horrible experience she had with my father. But this lifestyle did not come without its own difficulties. Quite a number of individuals in our small village would spend their time gossiping about Mum. I think she was viewed by some as a scarlet woman. We were only one of two families in our entire primary school to have divorced parents.

I sensed judgement from many who resided in our village. This was quite an ordeal for a little empath. I lacked the comprehension of abstract ideas such as empathy or judgement, but I sure felt these things strongly. As a result, I became more introverted, anxious, and always felt inadequate. These feelings stayed with me for many years alongside a deep concern for my mum, which manifested itself in many ways. One manifestation of this intense worry for Mum could be known today as obsessive-compulsive disorder. While I was at school each morning, during assembly, I would have to pray to God to look after Mum while I was not there to take care and watch over her. If I did not recite the prayer over and over, I would become even more anxious that something terrible would happen.

This was something I had to learn to overcome on my own. To add to this, I had just transferred to a new school for the third time and my new teacher terrified me. I had limited hearing in one ear and she also had hearing problems. For some reason, she took an instant dislike to me. Perhaps it was because I reminded her of her own impediment; or because I hid behind my little green and white stuffed rabbit that I brought with me to class; or because I did not bring her gifts like some of the other children did. Who knows? I was only six years old at the time and my first impression of school so far had been bleak.

Previously, I had been smacked twice on the back of my legs for not wanting to sit down on a grubby floor. That was my first day of school. Mum had told me not to get my new coat dirty.

Having a new coat was a real luxury and I was proud to wear my smart cream coat with the three chocolate brown buttons fastening it together. On entering the classroom, the teacher asked us to sit on the dusty parquet floor. My four-year-old mind instantly realized that I could not sit down or I would get my coat dirty. I lowered my eyes and bowed my head in the hope no one would notice me standing there when the sting of the hard slaps instilled fear into every cell of my being. This was the first time I had ever been hit. Neither Mum, nor my father, had ever hit me. For the shy, quiet, conscientious child I was, it was a huge shock which instilled fear and apprehension throughout my school years. Despite my efforts to be good and to be obedient to my mum, I had been punished. In that instant, I realized the duality in this third-dimensional reality, deepening the need for me to hide and not be seen.

At break, still reeling from the shock of being smacked, I snuck off of the school grounds and walked the half-mile to our home. Luckily, Mum was there to find me. She was furious. The teacher was reprimanded. Within twelve months of the incident, I had moved to another school where I settled well, until we moved houses and I changed schools, once more.

Mrs. F. threw our books at us as she yelled. I was so paralyzed with fear that I flat-out refused to go to school. Mum took the initiative to storm into the headmaster's office. Subsequently, I was moved to a different class, with a new, young teacher, whom I felt comfortable with straight away. She was kind to me and I soon eased into school life.

Overtime, I learned to deal with the thoughts I obsessed over and compulsive behaviors with the help of the Angels. I used to hear a loving and reassuring voice say: "don't worry, Tracey, your mum's well. She will be looked after while you are away." This positive affirmation soon replaced the fear-based constant prayer and I began to relax. My brother, on the other hand, became awkward and rebellious. He had a hard time dealing with all the insecurity and became quite a handful. I had a lot of empathy for him.

It was not until my teenage years that I fully understood why I had developed such anxiety as a small child. I was in my late teens when Mum informed me our local police officer, Harry, had died. "That's so sad!" I exclaimed. My heart and mind recalled how kind he had been. I explained to Mum that whenever I saw him walking around the village he always smiled and greeted me by my name. I used to see him with what my teenage mind could only describe as a gentle bright glow around his being. I learned as I got older that this was known as the Aura, or energy field, which emanates from a person. It has been scientifically proven that all objects and beings, humans included, have an electromagnetic energy field. The aura around a person consists of many colors. It can be close to the body or expand out a few feet. The color of the energy field changes depending on the mood of the individual.

Mum's mouth dropped open at this revelation and she proceeded to tell me what had happened when I was small. She said: "We had moved away from the home at Bunkers, not long after I separated from my boyfriend at the time. We went back to the village where your grandma lived and I rented a little cottage and started work as a barmaid just around the corner. There were plenty of children for you and Lee to play with. Although the majority were boys, this helped you toughen up a bit. I was dating Tony straight after the invisible man and I broke up and even though he cheered me up and gave me purpose, I became depressed and consumed a handful of tablets in an attempted suicide."

I had a recollection of this night over the years, although I could not quite remember the events or what it was about. I clearly remembered the sense of fear that something awful was happening as the police and neighbors rushed my brother and I out of the house. She went on to say: "I was newly divorced with another failed relationship with two children under the age of five. I was fed up and in a haze of despair, I saw a way out and took it while you and your brother slept. I started thinking about you both and felt an intense pang of guilt and regret. Within an instant of the thought of leaving you motherless in the same world I wanted out of, I dialed the number for the police to report what I had just done and cried for help."

It was Harry, the police officer, who had responded. He never forgot the trauma my family endured and never failed to show us compassion.

I then understood where my all-consuming childhood fear of losing my mum came from. I also understood why I saw Harry as a beautiful soul in the world even though I never really knew him. He saved Mum's life.

Tony, My First Stepdad

TONY WRAGG WAS AN EDUCATED MAN THAT ENJOYED COMPANY and outings. He had little interaction with us, to be honest, but did bring us more stability for a time. He met Mum shortly after she separated from the invisible man. By all accounts, they had a sweet and pleasant courtship. We often saw him walking up to the farm cottage we lived in with groceries for us and he would stay to share a drink with Mum. Tony took her to parties and outings to the local cricket club on sunny Sunday afternoons, which suited Mum's extroverted personality. Together, they also went rock climbing and had friends over often on evenings to play the card game, Bridge. They seemed compatible, as they were both outgoing and other adults found them fun to be around. Our home became a hangout for friends of Mum and Tony to frequently visit. I would see them gathered around the card table and the room would soon fill with their cigarette smoke and chatter. Tony was also a talented accountant. He did quite well for himself financially and could have done so much more. They married after four years of courtship when Mum found out she was pregnant with my younger sister, Sarah. Lee and I did not attend the ceremony; we would have been eight and seven years old at the time. Mum said they went with a witness to the local registrar's office due to the fact she was pregnant.

Tony spoke to me infrequently, if at all. He used to sing the song, "The Lord of the Dance", quite well at parties and he liked to eat curries and buttered onions that were wrapped in foil and baked in the oven. He did not like us to have any because he thought we would waste them, and he was probably right. I remember Mum telling him not to be so selfish. Tony was an only child and he had been well looked after by his parents. Mum would attribute his selfishness to him being an only child. When Mum and Tony had an argument or disagreement, he would remove the pocket money set aside for Lee and me from the mantle above the fireplace to show everyone that he was unhappy.

I did not think much of what it meant to have a new step-father until I was in school one day and we had to write our mother's name on the front of an envelope. Instant fear and anxiety once again overwhelmed me. *How could I write my mum's new name, which was different from mine? They will never know who she is.* I sat there staring at the letter and started to cry. My teacher at the time was understanding. Of course, they knew Mum's name had changed, but I was unaware that they knew. These were only little things to adults but could be significant experiences to children in times and places where second marriages were unusual.

But for all the awkwardness this marriage might have brought, I was blessed with a new grandfather. Grandad Tom, Tony's father, was filled with kindness. He loved and treated Lee and I as if we had been his biological grandchildren. He worked as a long-distance lorry (truck) driver and when he could he would take me for ride-alongs with him. I felt special sitting next to him so high up in the cabin. We did not speak much during these trips, both content to watch the road and country pass by through the window.

"I could take our Tracey anywhere. She is so well behaved." He would tell Mum when we returned. Hearing those words of approval meant the world to me. They gave me a confidence boost. The power of positive words can have such a huge impact. Positive words create positive energy.

One day at Grandad and Granny Wragg's, Lee and I were asked to come downstairs to eat. Lee threw one leg over the steep stair railing and slid all the way down to the bottom where

Granny Wragg was waiting for us. I went to copy him, sliding down on the handrail.

"Get down from there, please," Granny Wragg said. I slid all the way down, anyway. I had too much momentum to stop. But I never did it again after that. Lee did every time he came downstairs but there was never a time that she had asked him to stop. She ushered us to a small table in the living room to eat some lunch. While Granny Wragg had her back turned to us, Lee, sitting across from me, smirked at me. Seconds later, I felt the toe cap of Lee's shoe slam into my shin.

"Ouch!" I whined loudly, looking to see if Granny Wragg had noticed. I quickly flexed my knee, pulled my foot back as far as I could under the chair and swung it back towards my brother's shin. As soon as I connected, Lee cried out.

"Tracey, stop that," Granny Wragg said.

"I didn't start it, Lee did!" I protested.

"No, I didn't, Granny Wragg, Tracey kicked me," Lee tattled.

"No, he did not. Stop being sly and leave Lee alone," she scolded.

Another smile appeared on his smug face. From that day on I was considered "sly" by Granny Wragg and Lee could do no wrong in her opinion. Grandad Tom loved me, I could never understand why Granny Wragg did not like me much or why she always took Lee's side. In retrospect, Granny Wragg was observing the family dynamic through different eyes. While people often complimented Mum for my placid demeanor, Lee was always known for being a troublemaker. She must have noticed a difference in the way other adults responded to us. Being older than me, Lee witnessed more. Of course, this would have impacted his behavior. She had empathy for Lee. He needed someone on his side and she was the perfect person to share her love and protection. However, as a child, I saw their relationship as favoritism and believed Granny Wragg was just a fusspot.

Life with Tony as our stepdad settled down into a nice routine and I began to feel more secure and confident. My little sister, Sarah, was funny and cute. I adored her. Mum's time was spent working and taking care of us. I was allowed to play outside with my brother and all of the other children. We would collect conkers, play hide and seek, and many other games. We had a great time.

One of my favorite things to do was to go down to the pond to see if we could catch frogs or newts. On this particular summer day it was especially hot, about eighty degrees Fahrenheit. We had trekked down to the pond in a large group. The older children always watched out for me because I was the youngest. I dipped my fishing net in the pond and caught a little green frog. I popped him into my bucket with some pond water and a rock for him to sit on. I prided myself on taking care of him in the best way I could. We ran home and I showed my frog to Mum. Then, I placed the bucket on the window ledge so it would not get knocked over and the little frog would not fall out. We all decided to play a game. I was caught up in the moment when I heard an angelic voice say to me, "Tracey, your little frog needs water." I silently acknowledged the voice and thought that I would give him some more in a moment. I believed that he already had some, not taking into consideration how hot the day actually was. I carried on playing and a short time later I remembered what the angelic voice had said. I ran straight to the bucket and to my dismay the little frog had died. The water had all dried up. I was mortified. I was so sorry for neglecting the little frog. I then felt a loving presence wrap me in a blanket of love and reassurance and I heard the angelic voice in the most loving way say, "when you took the little frog from his home you became responsible for his life. We have to love and cherish all life, no matter how tiny that life may be." I might add that this was said with unconditional love, no judgement or criticism whatsoever. I have never forgotten this beautiful teaching. I gained a sense of knowing that all life is sacred and we can connect with all living beings when we are aware that it is possible. I cherish this valuable lesson and always try to give my best to all life. Many years later I wrote a children's story, "Ollie Bear's Adventures with the Rainbow Heart Light: The Little Green Frog", with the hopes of teaching whoever reads it that all life is sacred and inspiring others to respect the lives of all creatures.

On the day that Grandad Tom passed, I was waiting in the small sitting room at Granny Wragg's when Mum came down the stairs from the bedroom Grandad Tom was in. She gently explained to us that he had died. My heart sank, I felt this overwhelming sadness envelope me, nobody told us he was ill. It must have been their way of protecting us. Everybody dealt with their grief privately, nobody ever said anything else to me and Lee and we did not attend his funeral. Years later, I caught a glimpse of his spirit. I was walking home from school when half a mile in front of me an adult male was nearing the end of the road. He was about to turn the corner when he stopped, turned around, and smiled at me. I saw his familiar face as he rounded the corner. I ran to the end of the road and scanned the area with my eyes, but the street was deserted. He has also passed numerous messages to me through my intuitive friends.

A couple of years passed before Mum and Tony's relationship started to break down. They went through a nasty break-up after seven years together. Tony had continued to spend his money in the pub rather than on renovations to the house we had moved into two years prior, which desperately needed upgrading. We did not even have a bath installed. Tony was unable to drive past a pub without popping in for a pint or two (or three). There were a few occasions when I was left in the passenger seat of his red minivan in the carpark with a bottle of coke and a bag of crisps to keep me company while he would be in the pub. He swore me to secrecy. I hated sitting there, staring out at the car park. I still find it irritating to sit in the car waiting for anyone to this present day.

Mum had had enough of his false promises, which caused a huge rift between the two, leading to billiard balls being thrown through car windows and us children being ushered to Grandma Lily's in the dead of night. That same week I was asked to help Mum carry black bin bags of his belongings to Granny Wragg's, where he was staying. The feeling of anxiety once again arose as we took the bus to her home. The aftermath of the turbulent breakup reignited all of my previous insecurities, although this time, I had more emotional and mental strength and awareness. Only a few weeks after the breakup, Tony stopped by with a bunch of flowers in hand for Mum, and in front of Lee and I, he asked Mum for another chance, saying he would move us to a better home in a more desirable area. Before Mum replied, she looked at us, and asked if we wanted to move homes. Caught off guard and only ten and eleven years old, of course we said no, like any child would.

Then Mum told Tony: "That's your answer." I felt extreme guilt for my answer, I did not realize that by saying no to a new home, I was saying no to Tony.

I look back at the many happy times during this period of my life and I am eternally grateful to Tony and his parents. We were kept well while feeling secure and loved in the only way they knew how. I could probably count on my fingers the number of times that Tony and I had been in contact after they divorced. Mum and Tony became friends again in their mid-seventies after the breakdown of Mum's third marriage. This happened after I left the UK to live in California. On a recent visit to England, Tony asked Sarah if I would visit him. Sarah and I found this rather strange, if not bizarre. It was the first time he had ever asked to see me since their divorce. As it turned out during my whirlwind visit, I did not have the time to meet him. I was urged by my Angelic Friends to send him an abundance of unconditional love and positive healing energy to help him, not quite knowing why. It all became clear eighteen months later when the news came that he passed away. His higher-self must have sensed his time on the earth was limited and perhaps he wanted to clear some unfinished business between us before he left this realm, or unconsciously he knew that I could help him transition. The Angels confirmed this to me as my sister and I spoke via Skype. She then shared a beautiful poem he had written earlier. Sarah recorded him reciting it. His words were filled with light and I saw his beautiful heart. He was an old soul, one that had been hidden under the layers of shaded grey energy that many functioning alcoholics can carry.

Cobbler's Monday by Tony Wragg

I'm sure that Monday's not my style,
for working hands to bone,
I think that's why for quite a while,
I've walked the hills alone,
Until one day I met this lass,
she came from Milking Green,
and I was sure I couldn't pass,
the fairest one I'd seen.
I told her of the country way,
and much to my surprise,
she said she would come with me,
as she looked in my eyes,
So off we set one bonny morn,
I'm walking nine feet tall,
for on my own, I'm quite forlorn,
but not with her at all.
We climbed the brow to Scouthead top,
and moments lingered there,
it certainly was worth the stop, to see our hills so fair.
Then down the brow, for Dobcross bound,
we set a lively pace,

43

and drinking in the beauty 'round,
brought pleasure to her face.
By Nudger Green we chanced to see,
a poet of some fame,
I think that is what prompted me,
to write one to her name.
For Sandy Lane, we journeyed on,
and passed by Diggle's Mills,
where lonely lane wound through the glen,
towards these glorious hills.
So up and on towards the Church,
there was blossom in the air,
I think for miles you'd have to search,
to find a scene so fair.
Down Pickhill's fields we journeyed on,
the air was just like wine,
and Monday morn was almost gone,
I think we both felt fine.
Perhaps I'll walk another day,
and ask that lovely lass,
for that's the game, one ought to play,
to make dull Mondays pass.

The Boyfriend

Within a month of Mum and Tony's breakup, a new sense of peace filled our home. I was looking forward to spending time with Mum and my siblings without conflict. The commotion created by the divorce and the preceding fights between Mum and Tony had ended and I thought that the atmosphere of our home would be calmer and more enjoyable. My bubble soon burst.

Another weekend came and Mum had spent the day cleaning and organizing the home. She looked happy and was very upbeat. She thought it would be a good idea if we all played the board game, Monopoly. I was quite excited about this; it was out of character for Mum, she was never interested in playing Monopoly. Lee and I looked forward to having some excitement. While preparing the front room for our game night, Mum informed us that her "friend" would be joining us. I became suspicious and began to sense something felt off. My mum's new boyfriend stepped in the room and nervously sat down before us. I wanted to scream out, "what the hell are you doing, Mum? This is so wrong!"

Mum must have recognized the expression on my face as complete disgust and anger because she gave out a nervous little laugh. Every cell of my being knew this person was not meant to be close to our family. I felt like I was the adult and Mum was the wayward child in our relationship. How could I, at ten years old, convince Mum she was making a huge mistake. I was seething and felt extremely disappointed with her choice. I was unable to look at either one of them. This was unlike me, but the sense of something being off was too strong to ignore. The tension in the atmosphere of our home was a thick, hot, heavy fog. I did not like this man.

My fears and suspicions were soon to become reality. The following week, Mum informed us that he would be moving in. He was many years younger than her and had no experience with children. His family was nice and likable and his sister used to babysit us. Mum was unaware that she threw a lot of parties for her teenage friends while babysitting us at our house. Mum worked hard and the hours were long, as stewardess of the Conservative Club was a demanding position. Her new boyfriend would spend some time in the pub while Mum was working. On other occasions, he used to babysit us. I kept out of his way as much as possible. It was Lee who suffered the most. Her boyfriend used to bully Lee. Lee swore me to secrecy, and kept a lot to himself.

He said, "Tracey, I don't want to upset mum, she seems so happy. You can't tell her what's going on." I understood what he was saying, Mum had developed alopecia as a result of the stress caused by her divorce from Tony, and I agreed not to say anything, already feeling guilty for being the final straw that broke Tony and Mum's relationship. What I did not know was that her boyfriend was actually hitting Lee, regularly. Over the next three years concern for my brother grew. I could no longer turn a blind eye to how he was being treated.

During a fight I had with her boyfriend, I exclaimed, "you won't dare raise your hand to me because you know I will tell Mum!" He laughed at me and backed away. He seemed to think I was not a threat to him.

From Mum's recollection, shortly after this event, he accidentally slammed a door in my little sister's face and gave her a black eye. Everything came to a head. The truth came pouring out as I told Mum her boyfriend had not always been as good or nice to Lee as she believed. She was furious and kicked him out of the house. The next night after a day of drinking alcohol to drown his sorrows, he came into our home and sat me on his knee, proclaiming he would make love to Mum whenever he wanted to. In his drunkenness, he said he could do the same to me. I was terrified. Fortunately, Mum had been warned that he was en route to our home. She came running in with her new friend, Peter, in tow. Peter frog-marched him out of our home. I was so relieved and the fear diminished.

Years later, Sarah told me that once while he was bathing her, he had pushed her head under the water and held her there. She was five years old at the time. I knew from the moment he entered our home that there was no purpose for him in our lives or lessons to learn, only the potential to do harm. I wish I would have known the full extent of his treatment of Lee and had had the courage to tell Mum earlier. Our love and concern for her welfare prevented us from speaking out in Lee's defense. Maybe we could have averted this challenging time if we would have been brave enough to speak up. Another break-up might have been hard on Mum, but it was harder for her to know that her children had kept their experiences a secret for fear of upsetting her, and the treatment Lee endured had a lasting effect.

I am grateful and relieved he kept his darker shadow-side to a minimum. I know it could have been a lot worse and I thank his soul for controlling more harmful possibilities. I am sure we inadvertently helped him overcome a huge challenge within his own soul's journey. Upon writing this, I feel it is important to point out that there is a distinction to be made between having empathy, understanding, and forgiveness for others who have done wrong, and excusing harmful behavior. While I disapprove of his actions, I have total forgiveness for his soul. The fact that he kept it a secret from Mum showed he knew what he was doing was wrong and that was definitely not how to treat a young boy.

On Intuition

Dear Reader,

ALWAYS TRUST YOUR INTUITION. NO MATTER HOW OLD YOU ARE, your intuition is never wrong; it is a powerful guiding force. Intuition is the ability to sense things before they come into your reality. Some are born with a strong intuition and others have to learn to listen to the messages they receive. It may take many years to learn to trust in your intuitive side and perseverance is paramount. The more you trust, the stronger your intuition becomes.

First and foremost, stop your mental mind from overanalyzing what you may be perceiving. When you try to make sense of something that has yet to manifest in this physical reality, it is easy for the doubting mental mind to either disregard the perceived message or try to rationalize it; coming up with all sorts of scenarios and totally confusing the original intuitive hit, like adding two plus two and ending up with eleven. The key is to trust the message or feeling you receive and act accordingly.

How can we strengthen our intuition? The Angels have told me that many of us have a disconnect between the intuitive body and the mental mind. I have learned an analogy to understand intuition and how to strengthen it. I will teach it to you now:

Imagine a silver and gold line running from your heart to your head. When our intuitions are weakened, that line can become faint or even have a break in it. Strengthening the intuition is a process and does not happen instantly. When you get an intuitive hit, a feeling, message, or sign that causes you to know something without having an explanation as to why you know it, say to your mental mind: "I know you do not trust or understand the message, but for now take a back seat and observe." Wait to see if the intuitive side is right before trying to analyze it. When the reason for the intuitive hit comes to light and the feeling is validated, the mental mind begins to trust the intuitive body. If you continue to trust your intuition without first judging yourself or overanalyzing the feeling, and then, over time the mental mind learns to trust the intuitive side so much it lets it take the lead, strengthening the line of connection.

If you find your mental mind cannot take a back seat and you do not understand what you are perceiving, just stay neutral and observe. You can then become open to receiving the next piece of the puzzle, so to speak, or the next message or event which will help you to understand the previous one. Do not make any rash decisions; hold off until you see what starts to manifest and everything becomes clearer.

The exception to the rule is when you feel threatened or in peril. When there is danger close by your intuitive side screams at you to be aware. You may feel a deep sense of fear and your heart starts to pound for no obvious reason. Feelings of nausea in your solar plexus (just below your heart center) may appear in an inexplicable way that becomes so strong it feels like you have been physically punched in the gut. This feeling is not negative, it is your Guardian Angel alerting you to danger. Get away from the area you are in or from the person or persons you have just come into contact with. When feelings like these strike you, do not wait to gain any more clarity on the situation. Have blind trust and allow your intuition to protect you. Your spirit guides are talking to you through your senses and feelings.

There is a fine line between judgement and discernment. Many souls with compassionate hearts are sometimes frightened of judging another soul. They can become confused when sensing the truth about a situation that is not visibly obvious, thinking they are judging or criticizing and not being spiritual. The Angels cleared this up a long time ago with their simple explanation: "Intuition shows us the truth, we are not being judgmental when we are honoring truth. Honor your intuition, honor truth."

How do we distinguish intuition from fear? Intuitive bursts typically hit us in the present moment with a sense of neutrality, unless in danger, in which case feelings may be supercharged with emotion. Intuitive hits are hard to sense while lamenting over a problem. It is best to quiet or distract the mind during challenging times. I have used waking meditations to achieve an inner calm, thus, helping me to tune into the guidance I seek. This process clarifies my thoughts and emotions so that I am able to get through challenges with ease and grace. We have a choice to disregard an intuitive hit or to listen. The intuitive messages coming from our guardian Angels lend us a helping hand, especially in circumstances where we may have an incomplete picture. Many times, we disregard these messages because the logic-based mental mind cannot make sense or does not understand the message. Oftentimes fear arises in non–life-threatening situations when we have failed to quiet our minds. This is a sure way to block your intuition.

Is a suspicious mind the result of fear or intuition? Fear and suspicion go hand-in-hand. When a soul has a doubting or suspicious mind, they might view everything with distrust. This is not intuition. This is the mental mind going into overdrive through the fear of missing something it believes it needs to be aware of, which may be a coping mechanism for fear of being let down or taken advantage of or harmed in some way without an obvious cause to fear those things. This follows the thought process that if you never trust anyone, then you are never let down. The key is to strengthen the intuition enough that you can trust others and know your intuition will show you if something is off with them or the situation.

Intuition in Perilous Situations

It was 1972. Vic, who was only a child himself, had been babysitting his niece. After a long evening, he said his goodbyes and set off on the ten-minute walk to the bus stop. The night air was foggy. The misty dampness sent shivers up and down his spine. There was not another soul around. The soft glow of the lamp lights casting shadows all around added to the eerie atmosphere. Any child would have felt some apprehension. Vic zipped up his coat as far as it would go and tucked his dimpled chin under the warm fabric, pulled his bobble hat down over his cold ears and moved at a brisk pace, hoping the bus would be on time. He expected that the ride home would take twenty-five minutes and he was so tired he could not wait to climb into his cozy bed.

Vic was small for his ten years; yet, his personality was strong and fiery, like his taste in rock music. He reached the covered bus stop a little out of breath. The bus shelter had a roof and clear glass sides with a small plastic bench. Typically, the entrance to the bus stop is on the side of the pavement and the exit on the side of the curb, making it easy for everyone to form a queue. Vic entered the shelter and took a big sigh of relief. He went straight to the curb side in anticipation of the bus arriving any moment. All of a sudden, and for no apparent reason, he felt a strong sense of panic developing in the pit of his stomach. His mind did not understand it but the feeling persisted. A few moments later, an older male joined him in the bus shelter. Vic's panic continued, not knowing why, and he felt rooted to the spot.

From out of nowhere, the older male stated, "I will give you ten pence if you play with this."

Vic's feisty nature, fueled with adrenaline, gave him enough strength and courage to turn his head and yell, "fuck off and leave me alone!" His heart was pounding as he watched the perverted drunken man rise from the bench, not knowing if he was going to attack him. The man was so unnerved by Vic's boldness that he hurriedly left the bus shelter, leaving Vic alone, just in time for the bright orange double-decker bus to round the corner and pull up to the stop. Vic jumped on board, paid his fare, and sprinted to his seat. The aroma of stale cigarettes and beer rising from the bus floor never smelled so sweet and comforting.

I am confident that when Vic told the perpetrator to "fuck off" and leave him alone, Vic's spirit guide and the Angels created an energetic force so strong it frightened and shocked the stranger into leaving. Hopefully it scared him so much he never dared do anything like that again.

I encountered a similar warning from my intuition around the same age. While I was playing out with a group of friends, ages ranging from eight to ten years old, we encountered a strange man walking his dog. It seemed like he was following us. He never said a word but everyone in the group developed a deep sense of fear. Something about that man unsettled all of us. One of my friends said we need to get away from him and go home. We all ran home and told our mums. It was later confirmed that there had been a sexual predator in the area.

Children have strong intuitions when it comes to surreptitiously dangerous situations. We have to teach them to listen to their "gut instincts" and act on them, especially when they feel they are in danger but they cannot explain why they are feeling that way. Children need to feel they have a trusted adult that they can bring their problems to, without worry that they will be dismissed. Problems arise when they are taught to, above all else, respect all adults and authority, inadvertently subduing their intuition. While we can all fall under the assumption that another person's projection that everything is wonderful and perfect means it must be truly so, we should never ignore that niggle that says *something's not quite right with this person.* We do not have to look for the explanation to those feelings; we can simply keep ourselves and our more vulnerable loved ones at a safe distance.

I know several friends, acquaintances, and clients who had been unintentionally put in harm's way during childhood because the adults responsible for their care believed another person to be good or spiritual. One such incident happened when an unsuspecting family deeply trusted their local priest. He became a big part of their family and even lived with them for a short time. Unbeknown to the adults, he had groomed and sexually abused one of their young children. The adults were blinded and would not hear a bad word said about the priest. The child, witnessing the adults' love for their abuser, felt totally alone and kept quiet for the longest time in the fear that they would not be believed. Eventually, one of the adults noticed something was wrong with the child's behavior, became suspicious, and after reassuring the child that they were safe to speak up if something was upsetting them, the truth came out.

As we have a responsibility to protect our own children, so do we have a responsibility of protecting the forgotten child, that is, the child with no one to trust. Brought more and more into light over the years, thanks to organizations like Operation Underground Railroad, is the plight of the forgotten child, alone, abandoned, and abused. By being vigilant and aware of the signs of the forgotten child, the one who has been thrust into a life of abuse by dark-hearted souls, we can shine a light on them and their dire situation and they will know they have not been forgotten after all.

While discussing children and intuition with my dear friend, Michelle, she shared an experience from many years prior about how she approached the topic with her own child. It was Christmas, 1998. Michelle and her five-year-old daughter were holiday shopping at the Laguna Hills Mall in Orange County,

California. In typical holiday cheer, Christmas music played loudly over the mall sound system. Large ornaments and garlands hung from the walls and ceiling, and people shuffled in and out of boutiques and department stores. While Michelle and her daughter were passing between shops, a man approached the pair. With a big smile on his face, he enthusiastically grabbed her arm in an attempt to usher her towards the nearby mall exit, asking her to accompany him to the parking lot, where he would show her some puppies waiting in the back of his car. Not wanting to frighten her daughter, Michelle calmly and firmly replied, "no, thank you. I am not interested," as she pulled her arm back from his grasp. She scooped her daughter into her arms, pushed past the man, and found a space she felt safe in towards the back of a Hallmark shop. Amidst the colorful decorations, countless cards, and charming gifts, she sat her daughter down. She crouched down to meet her daughter at her level, looked into her eyes and noticed the worry in them. Michelle asked her daughter, "are you okay?"

In a fearful tone, her daughter said, "Mommy, I didn't like the way that man made me feel." Michelle asked her what it was that she had felt and her daughter replied, "I felt a very bad feeling in my stomach."

Maintaining eye contact, Michelle said in a stern manner, "never forget that feeling. That is your intuition. And I had a bad feeling about that man, as well."

While it might have seemed appropriate for a parent to reassure their child that all was well and that there was nothing to fear, Michelle instead used this unsettling moment as a learning experience for her daughter. Michelle confirmed that her daughter's feelings were valid and reinforced that she was within her right to express those feelings and act on them if she needed to do so. Thus, teaching her five-year-old child that the strong feeling she had in her stomach was her intuition, which would always alert her to dangerous people or situations.

After some time in the Hallmark store, Michelle and her daughter left the shop and found security personnel, who escorted them safely to their car. A few days later, Michelle heard from local news sources that there had been several women targeted at the Laguna Hills Mall by a man using the same guise. Sadly, some of these ladies had fallen for this predator's spiel and became victims of sexual assault.

When emotions are high or one is in a compromised situation, as illustrated by Vic and Michelle's stories, both were able to react quickly and avert danger because they listened to their intuitions. Distinguishing between intuition and fear is somewhat more difficult when in a more controlled environment and when given more time to think one's feelings through. This next example is a mixture of intuition and my own fears.

When I was in my early thirties, I had been asked to go to the home of one of my regular clients to give thirty-minute readings to a few of her friends and relatives. During one of these sessions, I got a sense that something was wrong, not with the lady sitting before me, but with one of her close relatives. I was given a name by my guides and I asked her if that name meant anything to her. It was her brother's name. In a matter of seconds, the words, "tell him to keep his hands off of those children," flew out of my mouth. The message came from her deceased mother. We locked eyes and for a brief moment time stood still. I was in no doubt the message was the truth. After we got over the shock the message brought to both of us, she went on to explain that her brother had just been accused of inappropriately touching his girlfriend's two small children and that he had not done anything wrong. The police had let him go because there was no evidence. She asked me what her mother thought. Once again, the words came flying out, "he touched them."

She took the news as well as she could and shared that she had her own doubts and she would tell him to seek professional intervention. While wrapping up the session, all I could think was

Peter, My Second Stepdad

I LIKED PETER FROM THE VERY FIRST MOMENT I SET EYES ON HIM as he had saved me from what could have been a dangerous situation. He had been raised as an only child and was ten years younger than Mum. I thought that, despite the age difference, he would be good for her. I think she was relieved that her intuitive thirteen-year-old daughter got a good vibe from him. Peter moved into our home within a few months of our first meeting. He even took me shopping and bought me a silver heart-shaped Saint Christopher necklace. The affectionate gesture touched my heart. Not long after, Mum asked if she could talk to me about something important. Her words were: "What would you think if Peter and I had a baby soon?"

I replied: "I'd be fine about it." I had presumed that they would be trying to conceive in the near future.

A couple of weeks later, while sitting on the bus on my way home from school my friend asked, "Tracey, what do you think about your mum having a baby at her age? It's horrible, isn't it?"

Aghast, I exclaimed, "Mum's not pregnant!"

My friend said, "oh, yes she is! My mum and dad were talking about her."

I was so embarrassed and upset by the village gossip that I jumped off the bus at the next stop, ran home, and confronted Mum.

"I told you we were going to have a baby," Mum said.

"You could have told me you were actually pregnant!" I replied.

Mum and Peter married before my baby sister, Maria, was born. She was a sweet soul and it was my job to babysit her twice a week while Mum and Peter spent nights socializing and playing the card game, Bridge. It was at this time I began tapping into my creative side. I found that embroidering helped me relax. Focusing on the little different stitches and colored threads brought me right to the present moment. I was not thinking about the past or the future. This was a waking meditation. I had not realized this at the time, it just felt good. I would spend hours creating little plaques as family gifts and embroidering motifs on little pillow cases for my baby sister's pram.

Waking meditations calm my mind and distract me from anything that may be causing disharmony within. During waking meditations, I focus on the task at hand, not allowing my mind to become distracted with mental chatter. If I am driving, I only think about driving. If I am washing dishes or doing household chores, I am only thinking about the dishes or the chores. While walking on the earth on my own, I pretend my mind resides in my feet and, of course, my feet do not think. I then visualize my feet planting the light of Unconditional Love with every step I take. All waking meditations bring me right to the present moment and you know what they say about the present moment? It is a Gift. All of these waking meditations bring peace to my heart and they are easy. I try to apply waking meditation to many of the ordinary things I do in everyday life. It is essential for my wellbeing and in helping me retain a peaceful equilibrium within.

There are many types of meditation which have been proven to be great stress relievers. One of the easiest ways to start is by guided meditation. During guided meditation listeners are led by a narrator, either in person or via an audio device. The latter allows people to meditate in the comfort of their own homes. In a guided meditation, the narrator takes you through the process step-by-step, often by bringing attention to your breathing and setting the scene, giving you something to focus on, thus amplifying your relaxation. Another easy way to meditate is to focus on an object. I like to focus on the flame of a candle.

Candle Light Meditation

LIGHT A CANDLE, PREFERABLY ONE IN A GLASS JAR, AND PLACE IT on a heat resistant surface away from anything flammable. (Believe it or not, one of my clients set fire to her kitchen curtains when she placed her candle too near the window. Safety first.) Make yourself comfortable. Take three deep breaths. As you breathe in, think to yourself: *relax*. As you breathe out, think to yourself: *release*. Know all of your troubles and woes are being transformed into bright lights of positive energy. Continue to take deep breaths in and out. Feel totally and utterly relaxed, safe and comfortable in the knowledge that you are being held in the light of the Divine. Bring your attention to the candle flame. Watch it dance. Focus on the color. If your thoughts start to wander, bring your attention back to this little fire dance. After a while your eyes may become heavy. Let them close and focus on the flame in your mind's eye. Allow feelings of peace and well-being to permeate every cell of your being. When you are ready to come back into awareness, wiggle your fingers and toes. Stretch your arms and legs a little and open your eyes.

This is just another example of a meditation technique. Find the technique that is right for you. There are many available on the web, in audiobooks, and in print. I have included several techniques that have served me well throughout the years towards the end of this book. Audio downloads of these meditations will be made available on my website: Www.theRainbowHeartLight.com.

The Ghost

PETER WAS A GOOD MAN WITH QUITE A FEW QUIRKS. HE NEVER yelled at us, but would do little things in the only way he knew how to bring structure and organization to our family. He would take the plug off my hairdryer if I forgot to put it away; he would remove the lightbulb from my bedroom if I forgot to turn the light off; and he would use tie wraps to keep my curtains closed if I forgot to run upstairs straightaway after arriving home from school and draw the curtains in my bedroom to keep the heat in. This form of structure came from his own strict upbringing and his number of years in the Grenadier Guards Band, where he had to be organized and structured. He had become a father to four children in the space of a year, which was no easy feat. Even though Peter could be strict and have rules that I might not have liked, I learned to respect and appreciate him. I felt safe with him. He worked incredibly hard to provide a good and stable home for our family. I knew he was working his way through a huge life change in the best way possible, just like the rest of us. It certainly is not easy being a stepparent or a stepchild.

Within a year of meeting Peter, we had moved into a home in Greenfield that was built in the 1960's. It was an attached, three-bedroom house in a row of five dwellings. From the moment I stepped foot in it, I knew there was something wrong with that house. The atmosphere often felt smothering, cold, erratic, and antagonistic.

Life with Peter was busy. Mum and Peter had started doing odd jobs around the home, pouring their hearts and souls into making it a cozy space for all of us. We had not lived there long when Lee began to act out more. He was argumentative and disruptive. Peter and Lee did not get along and one day Peter reached his limit. Lee arrived home drunk late one night while the rest of us were sleeping and nearly burned the house down while attempting to make chips in a deep fryer. Peter said he had to leave. Lee's constant nitpicking and name calling towards me had intensified during this period. In one way his leaving was a relief and, in another way, I felt sad for him. He was only sixteen years old and all of the past trauma he had endured from so many different sources had a huge impact on him. Counseling had not been an option at the time, we were not even aware of it in our part of the world. In Peter's mind, he was protecting the rest of the family. Being only a young man himself, he did not have the experience or knowledge to deal with Lee's behavior in any other way and Lee would not have known how to ask for help to deal with his negative emotions.

Mum managed to arrange a rented flat just around the corner of our home for Lee to live in. We all helped decorate it and he soon settled down. At the same time the earthbound resident in our new home started to make his presence felt. Unbeknown to us, we were living with a manipulative spirit. This would have affected everyone, influencing our moods and impressing their feelings on to the most vulnerable members of our family, causing disturbance wherever possible. Perhaps this spirit was partly responsible for my brother's increasingly turbulent behavior, subconsciously feeding the spirit's anger and frustration, thus magnifying his own. I do believe this is exactly what happened. As tensions heightened around the home, a vicious cycle of fear and anger ensued. This fed the discarnate spirit, allowing it to become stronger and stronger, until a profound intervention from our Angelic Friends eased the troublesome extra burden placed on our shoulders

Picking up feelings from people and seeing things that most people could not, was something to which I had already become accustomed. I did not understand why it was happening and

I was too shy and embarrassed to ask anyone for help, so I just accepted that this was how my life would be. How was I supposed to tell my family about the stranger's face that stared back at me as I gazed out the third story window of the old Victorian hospital? How could it have benefited me to share with my friends that I heard voices they could not—or that I knew things that I could not explain? My reality was somewhere centered in the layers of past, present, and future. I did not think it would help me at all to share these things. The only one I could tell was Mum.

There was a gravity in the home that would not subside and I had developed new feelings of the fear and paranoia of being watched. I always slept with the hall light on and my bedroom door open. One night while in this house, as I slept, I awoke to the sharp sensation of fingers poking into my ribs. I could find no physical evidence to explain why I was being poked in my ribs so I told myself to ignore it as I usually did when this sort of thing happened. Overtime, what I suspected to be a ghost, began manifesting itself into shadows that would follow me around the house. I could see its darkness creeping. I began to sense the Ghost was an older male. I was frightened and he wanted me to be. He was the most aggressive at night. Many nights I would hear his footsteps as he walked up the stairs to my room. Many nights he would kneel beside my bed, breathing into my ear. On one occasion, I felt a weight placed on my torso and the sensation of being pressed down until I could not breathe. I could no longer ignore what was happening to me. I explained to Mum what was going on and I would cry out for it to stop. Mum began to pray for me even though she was an atheist. It was all the makings of a scary movie, except when a scary movie was over most people could leave the theater, go home, and tell themselves it was just a story and that sort of thing never happened in real life. Most people did not fall asleep to feelings of an invisible stranger's breath on their ear.

The night that I had finally struck the wall of my emotional and psychological limitations, I fought back my tears and struggled through my exhaustion to pray. I could feel his rasping breath on my face, and see his dark and looming shadow. I felt it would never end and this, too, would just be a part of my life.

"Dear God," I begged, "I can't do this anymore, I am so scared. Make him stop. I'm so scared. Please help me," I prayed. For a few seconds I heard only my own terrified heart beating before the menacing whispers and sounds continued. Was he going to touch me? Poke me? Sit on me? Smother me? Or worse?

They heard me. I knew the Angels had heard my cry for help. A flood of warm peace rushed over my body, as if a large warm blanket had risen over the foot of my bed and settled down on top of me. It was followed by the sensation of being cradled. I felt that my body had been immersed in a cocoon of liquid golden light. It filled every part of my mind and my heart. This light sent me instantly into a dream. Waiting for me in my dream was an Angel and gently resting in this Angel's arms was a big white Persian cat. The Angel passed the fluffy guardian over to me while gently whispering, "he will sit with you every night, protecting you while you sleep." I had just experienced the divine love and calmness of the Angels and I knew from that moment that I was safe.

In the morning, I found Mum in the kitchen. She looked up at me from the table with doubting eyes.

"It's going to be okay now, Mum," I told her with sincere confidence. I told her what I had dreamt the night before and that the menacing breathing and touching had stopped. I promised her that I was not scared anymore. She leaned towards me and reached out to where I was standing. From my nightgown she plucked a single, thumb-length, thick, white hair. We had no pets. We looked at each other in amazement.

Even though I could still sense his presence around the house, the lost soul never bothered me again. Although life was not without challenges, I found a new sense of confidence and growing peace in my heart knowing I was divinely protected.

Many years later, as an adult in full knowledge and awareness of my gifts, I decided it was high time that I helped the lost soul transition to the light, not only for the sake of his soul, but for the present and future occupants of the property.

On driving by my former residence, I felt chilled to the bone as I recalled the scary memories from my young teenage years. I reassured myself that there was nothing whatsoever to be afraid of. When we fear, we give the lost discarnate souls more energy. Thoughts create energy. If our thoughts are in fear, oppression, anger, and resentment, the discarnate soul can feed off of it, thus becoming empowered and creating more mischief, perpetuating the cycle of terror.

Always remember: Nothing from the spirit world can harm you unless you believe it can. When facing an energy you perceive as dark energy, keep your thoughts loving and positive. In doing so, your loving energy acts as a beacon of light, helping you pass swiftly through the darkest of shadows.

I circled back around and parked the car outside my old home. It was time for me to face my fear and stand in the light of Unconditional Love and positive healing energy to help the lost soul move on. After a few moments of quieting my mind and connecting with The Benevolent Angels of Light, I sensed his presence. He was angry, resentful, frightened and reluctant to leave. I knew my mission would not be easy as he had been stuck on this earthly plane for a long time.

He remembered me and knew that this time I was in complete control. He could not harm me in any way. On this realization, I felt his overwhelming sadness and disappointment. He had lost his power and his guard had come down. It was the perfect moment to start conversing. I asked him why he had not left when he originally died. He was reluctant to share anything at first. I gently persisted and got the impression he had always been depressed, bitter, lost and lonely. He told me that when he was alive, he hated his family. They had been estranged for many years and never made peace before he passed. He went through a miserable time suffering from mental illness and had died alone by his own hand. I found out years later that a man had taken his own life in the home and his body was not found until some time had passed. All of this antagonized his confused spirit so much he refused to go to the light when the Angels of Transition beckoned, instead choosing to become earthbound. Tormenting the living gave him a sense of power and worthiness. This was something he had never felt in the physical and it became quite an addiction for his lost soul.

I asked him if he thought his behavior was to blame for the alienation of his family. He became angry with me poking at this large raw nerve. This was the key I needed to help him transition. After a few minutes, his anger started to subside and he allowed the light of positive healing energy to wash over him, healing the sadness, anger, self-hate and frustration that had been emanating from his heart center. I gently reassured him that if he left this realm, and went to the light, all would be forgiven. I encouraged him to forgive himself for all of his past negative behavior. "How could I ever do that?" he cried.

I replied, "I forgave you a long time ago, and I'm sure everyone else will, too." He asked how I or anyone else could forgive him. I said it was possible with understanding and unconditional love in our hearts. I felt an overwhelming sense of Angelic Love enveloping his soul as I continued to reassure and encourage him to step into the light when guided.

I took a moment to visualize a vertical beam of golden white light filled with the energy of unconditional love, peace, and joy. The Angels brought his mother into the light to greet him. It was now time to persuade him to go. He was hesitant at first but with a gentle nudge he stepped in. I could see his eyes light up with the glow of love as he saw his mother's nurturing, forgiving, and loving presence. She immediately embraced her long lost son. Before they left, I heard him whisper, "Thank you."

Different Types of Visitations: Lost Souls

Discarnate souls, souls with a former life on earth that are no longer attached to a body, are capable of displaying many emotions. Such spirits may retain a lot of their former earthly personalities, positive or negative, and are capable of feeling emotions such as love, joy, anger, guilt and regret. Some can be quite helpful and loving, even alerting you to any danger and protecting what they consider "their property"; they like to help their earthly tenants. Others are sad, frustrated, and angry, causing mayhem like the spirit in my prior encounter.

Some recently deceased souls do not even realize that they have died. They become suspended between two realities. These are rare instances where they either cannot or will not accept that they have passed on. The majority of souls passing over, traumatic or not, do so with ease.

The rare occurrence of an earthbound discarnate soul can be due to a sudden traumatic death, unfinished business with loved ones, or other unresolved conflicts including those disputes tied to feelings of guilt. These earthly concerns leave the soul without peace or rest, stopping them from coming to terms with their own deaths and moving on to the light of Unconditional Love. One of my first experiences with a soul that was unaware of her own death happened many years ago.

When Oliver, my son, was five years old, he had a playdate with his new school friend. I was happily chatting with his friend's mum when I sensed the spirit of a distraught teenager. I asked her if she knew a young lady who had recently taken her own life. She went white in the face and began to explain that a close family friend had died in this manner the week before. She went on to say that the family had been feeling a strong presence in their home: doors banging, lights flickering on and off. They were deeply concerned for the soul of their loved one.

I communicated with the young spirit. She was relieved that I could see and hear her. She had not been able to understand why nobody else could; this was driving her crazy. She thought she was still alive and in some kind of altered reality. She had been creating as much noise as possible in the hope of attracting their attention. I gently explained to her she had passed over. At first, she did not believe me.

"Really?" she asked.

"I'm sorry, yes," I answered as gently as before. I explained: "you need to go to the light with the Angels. Then, you can come back and visit your loved ones when the time is right.

When the reality had set in that she had indeed passed, she started to sob and exclaimed, "I didn't mean to kill myself! It was just a cry for help!" With this statement she was immediately bathed in a beautiful golden glow. She said, "tell them I'm sorry," as she transitioned to the light. This young lady was depressed and wanted her family to understand her pain. Sadly, she lost control of her cry for help and, in doing so, also lost her life.

Most souls make the crossing into the afterlife effortlessly. However, there are also souls that consciously choose not to transition. Other entities prefer to stay in a physical reality that they are familiar with. Some like to be guardians of places they are attached to or have some significance to them and choose to stay. Others may fear going to the light. This seems quite unbelievable; how can anyone fear the light of Unconditional Love? I have found that the fear of being judged for past actions by a greater power can be so big that some souls tend to hide or refuse to go when the Angels of Transition beckon. Once they are convinced that the light is all loving they will move on.

I recall a wonderful experience with such a discarnate soul in the late 1990's. I had been asked to walk around an old theater that had a reputation for having an awful lot of paranormal activity by a woman conducting research on the building and her camera crew. Visitors in the theater had experienced touches on their shoulders by unseen hands and heard heavy breathing. Some of the staff had witnessed items being moved without explanation. The old theater, built in the early 1900's, was steeped in history. I stepped into the foyer; the atmosphere felt warm and inviting. I found a quiet space to prepare myself to observe the energy in the building. After a few minutes of silence, I began to sense and single out the unseen force causing a lot of the paranormal activity. I opened myself up to communicate.

After a few moments, a strong spirit appeared right before my face and instantly began to relay his messages: "I am the caretaker of this theater and I'm not giving up my position for anybody!" he asserted. "They wanted me to leave my position," he continued passionately, "I was angry, hurt, and confused. What had I done to deserve being fired?" Then, he explained to me how he had come to die. "In a fit of rage and despair," he said, "I hung myself." He was aware that he was in spirit form, but had so many strong ties with the theater, which was the place of his work and his death, he did not want to leave. Entities like the caretaker of the theater can be difficult to interact with. They consider themselves to still be a part of their environment, causing them to become territorial, often appearing angry, frightened, or confused, especially when they feel threatened. This can cause them to scare the living. He felt comfortable with our connection and decided that he wanted to show me around the theater.

We proceeded to walk every inch of the old theater. He would stop me at certain spots to share information. While walking up the aisle alongside an outer wall he said, "this is where the entrance used to be." He then mentioned that the restroom we were about to enter was not a part of the theater and exclaimed loudly, "you won't like it in there, it's not nice!" We went into the restroom; boy, was he right: the energy in this small lady's restroom was awful. I sensed a totally different entity; one I chose not to converse with. I also felt there had been some terrible event that had left a residue of energy from the past. I left the restroom quickly. I was told afterwards that many guests had been touched inappropriately by an unseen force while visiting that rest room. I asked the Angels to clear this awful energy and moved on. We proceeded on our tour. I sensed a few other visitors but had no other interactions. The caretaker informed me that he was still the one in charge.

Eventually, we arrived at the stage where the caretaker said he had hung himself. I sensed the pain and sadness this poor man had felt in his last moments. I wrapped this lost soul in a loving healing energy and persuaded him to go with the Angels to the light of Unconditional Love. I said to him, "go and see if you would like it." I knew that if he went, he would not want to come back to this physical reality. He agreed to go and left the theater, his pain, and his anger for good.

The manager had been researching the history of the theater for over twenty years. He confirmed everything the caretaker had shared and was blown away by the accuracy of the details. The manager said, "this information took me years to gather and it took you an hour."

In the example of the caretaker of the theater, the lost soul decided to go on to the next life and leave his past behind. In my experience, this is not always the case. In 2018, Vic and I stayed at the historic fifteenth century hotel, The George and Pilgrims, in Glastonbury, England. We would come to find on this trip that the hotel offered more than just a comfortable bed and good food. We arrived weary after a long journey from California. As I was picking up the keys and walking up the ancient winding staircase to our room, all I could think about was sleep. Vic put the key in the lock, the door swung open, and we instantly felt the ice-cold energy waiting for us. We knowingly looked at one another, put our bags down, freshened up, and climbed into bed. Just before resting my head on the pillow, I stated quite firmly to the ghostly energy: "please do not disturb me tonight, I am way too tired. I will talk to you in the morning." Within seconds, Vic saw a bright blue orb about four inches in diameter move over me to the other side of the room. Vic was quite excited to see this wonderful phenomenon as I was falling asleep. I shushed him and told him to go to sleep, too.

After a great night's sleep, I woke up promptly at 5:00 AM. As agreed, I began to converse with the many spirits waiting eagerly to tell their stories: a monk, a woman I perceived to be a nun or in some way connected to a monastery (but not quite a nun because of her strange head garment), a second woman, and a little boy. The monk and the little boy came through in a particularly strong way. I listened keenly. The monk and the woman, the one I connected to a religiously affiliated role, had been caught together in a clandestine meeting. They could not disprove the accusations that they were lovers and both succumbed to a horrible death. I was overcome with the feeling of being unable to move or breathe while they gave me a sense of their passing. Intense feelings of shame and sadness prevented these distressed souls from moving to a higher realm. They indicated to me that they had created quite a bit of mischief with many of the hotel's guests, usually if they felt disrespected by the living. While listening to their stories, I had asked the Angels to surround them with the light of Unconditional Love and positive healing energy to help heal and release all of their past trauma. A wave of peace washed over the room. They just wanted their story to be heard. All souls have free will, so I gently asked if they would like to leave and go to the light. They happily decided to stay, promising they would not frighten anyone anymore. Although, I felt they would show themselves from time to time.

The little boy was quite a joyful soul. He told me he had worked in the kitchen with his mother and was now a custodian of this special space. I thanked them for making us feel comfortable. I can honestly say I had never slept better.

Vic and I decided it was time to rise and head downstairs for breakfast. The friends we were traveling with joined us at the table. After a lengthy chat and a nice meal, I popped back up to our room to change my footwear. While walking up the small staircase, a gentleman, named Joseph, who worked at the inn greeted me and promptly asked which room I was staying in.

I replied: "7 Abbott Whiting." He asked about my thoughts on the room. I explained my experience from earlier that morning. He was not at all surprised. After I introduced him to Vic and our friends, he offered to show us around the hotel the following morning. We gratefully accepted and proceeded to go out for the day, walking up to the Tor, Chalice Well, and many other wonderful ancient sites. On descending the Tor, we noticed quite a number of sheep grazing on the right-hand side of the field and one quietly sat off to the left on her own. I thought to myself perhaps this one is a rainbow sheep, one unafraid to stand out. Then, out of the blue, our friend, Pablo, asked me to take a picture of the solitary sheep. I willingly obliged and was pleasantly surprised to see a magnificent rainbow confirming my prior thought. I also sensed it was a message to us all: "Do not be afraid to be your authentic genuine self; consequently, gaining confidence and allowing your colorful light to shine bright."

Our next stop was Chalice Well, also known as the Red Spring. This is one of Britain's most ancient holy wells, situated between Glastonbury Tor and Chalice Hill. It is surrounded by the most beautiful and blissful gardens. I found the energy to be strong and pure, regenerating and revitalizing my whole being. As I drank the healing waters, feelings of strength, peace and inspiration coursed through my mind, body, and soul. While meandering through the gardens, observing and listening to the sparkly trickle of water, I was urged by my spiritual guides to take a picture. I noticed a blue heart formed by the light and trees, a heavenly confirmation from this sacred space.

After an action-packed day, we headed off on a two-and-half hour car drive to meet relatives for dinner and drop our friends off in London. The pleasant evening ended, we said our goodbyes, and set off back to Glastonbury. The drive back took us down country roads that were dimly lit, tree-lined, and winding. I looked at Vic and noticed a smile on his face. "What's going on?" I asked.

"I've started to see this vibrant magenta light like a mist in the trees. It feels like I am driving in a tunnel of pink and violet light. I just feel a warm sense of peace and calm," he admitted.

"How beautiful!" I exclaimed. "You are seeing beyond this reality."

We eventually arrived back to the eerily quiet George and Pilgrims in the early hours of Saturday morning. As we were walking down towards the back door, I once again heard, "take a picture." Wondering what was to appear this time, I readied my phone and opened the camera application to capture another image. Lo and behold! The Shadow of the sweet little boy came into sight in the patio window. I thanked him for showing himself and we silently climbed into bed and went to sleep.

Saturday, 9:30 AM sharp, we met with Joseph for what we thought would be a five-minute tour of the hotel's cellar. Our guide had other plans. He told us his friend would also be joining us shortly. The three of us went down into the cellar of the hotel. I sensed the spirit of the monk again. He was trying to show me a previous passage that was now blocked up. Joseph confirmed that a monk was believed to have been bricked up in the wall for breaking his vow of chastity. This made perfect sense with what I had perceived on the first morning we arrived. We left the cellar and explored the lobby and dining area where we were greeted by his friend Siobhan. She was dressed in a long flowing, forest-green cape, holding a wooden staff with the carving of Capricorn's head atop.

After a warm introduction, Vic and Siobhan dove into a deep conversation with one another. I got the sense that she was a master of time and space, having the ability to move in many different dimensions with ease and grace. Joseph and I continued to check out the many rooms recently vacated. What struck me as strange was that every time we walked past Vic and Siobhan they were still in deep conversation while he stood intently holding the staff with both hands, in exactly the same spot as we had left them.

Continuing through the rooms, I sensed energetic activity in all but one. I lost count of the number of spirits I met. Joseph, knowing the place and being an intuitive himself, confirmed much of the information I had relayed. I then came across another extremely distressed soul. She was screaming at me. She shared her horrendous story of loss, rape, and murder. When her story was finished, she experienced a release of her emotions and pain. She then was finally able to move into the light of Unconditional Love and peace. Others, like the monk, chose to stay. This unexpected work was now complete. I felt blessed and honored to have been able to help these souls in any way possible.

Joseph and I went back to the lobby and I could not help but smile on noticing Vic still holding the staff. He had not moved from the same spot for over two hours. I joined them, and Siobhan invited me to hold the staff. The energy from the staff pulsated and vibrated. With my eyes closed, I saw a glimpse into many different dimensions. When I opened my eyes, Siobhan brought her face close to mine and stared into my eyes. She asked me: "Do you know who I am?" I did. She had been overshadowed by the energy of an Archangel. Then she said, "I am Uriel."

I had remembered what was said to me three days prior to leaving on this trip. While working with one of my more intuitive clients, she blurted out, "Tracey, watch out for Archangel Uriel. You need to connect with Archangel Uriel."

As Victoria and I were discussing this chapter, a golden oriole tapped on the window three times, and appeared again a fourth time. Golden orioles are associated with Archangel Uriel, spreader of God's light of truth into places of darkness and confusion. Archangel Uriel is associated with the cardinal directions, space and time.

Vic had also been on quite the trip. Siobhan said he was a master shaman and was direct with his insight. Vic described traveling to different dimensions and locations on earth in accurate detail, including that Siobhan had a doppelganger, an unrelated exact double living in another part of the world, in New Zealand, which she confirmed. His experience was similar to astral projection. While not leaving his body, he allowed his mind to go, knowing his feet were firmly planted on the grounds of that hotel, rooted to the spot with Capricorn, the talking stick. When I relayed this story to Barbara, my dear friend of many years, she and I jokingly asked Vic if he would like to take over some of our responsibility as intuitives.

He laughed and graciously declined.

The spirit of the little boy at the patio window in the George and Pilgrim, Glastonbury, England.

The Angels

The word Angel means messenger or harbinger. They are benevolent beings of the highest sense, shining bright light into our earthly realm. Their energy mark is one of vitality and wellbeing. They do their best to keep us from harm's way and bring messages of love, comfort, peace and truth. Sharing their wisdom and raising the vibration of our senses, they inspire and encourage us to be our most virtuous authentic loving selves. They help us to heal the cellular memory and remind us of the pure essence of love, truth and goodness that exists within everything.

I have seen the magnificent Archangels many times, especially Archangel Michael. He appeared to me when I first awakened, infusing me with a bright blue light of love and strength, reassuring me there was nothing I could not overcome on my path. I have seen Raphael's beautiful healing emerald green light bestowed onto many during health crises. Most recently, I had an encounter with Uriel, known as the light of God.

Archangel Gabriel is portrayed holding a trumpet and is known as the patron saint of communication and the messenger of truth. Archangel Gabriel is constantly helping me to overcome my fear of being seen, giving me courage and strength to convey my messages to the world. While writing this, Victoria reminded me of her experience with Gabriel the day she met me.

I had been invited on a girl's trip to Las Vegas. Oliver informed me that morning as I was waiting for my ride that his girlfriend of a few months was driving down from Ventura County to spend the day with him and would like to say hello and introduce herself to Vic and I if she had the opportunity. About two minutes before my friend arrived to pick me up, Victoria (Vicky) appeared in a Jeep with her best friend at the wheel and jumped out quickly. She nervously and excitedly greeted Vic and I with a hug and a smile and introduced her friend to us. My friend pulled up to the apartment and I was whisked away to Las Vegas soon after.

That night, back at home with her parents, while trying to go to sleep, her room was filled with a white light and a voice of a being she only saw as energy. The being introduced himself as the Angel Gabriel and showed Vicky a memory of herself as a child. He relayed many messages and images to her, including images of her and Oliver many years down the road. Vicky was struggling to get along with her parents at the time, as teenagers often do. She was told about the goodness that lives within them and was shown to both admire and respect them for their sincere love for humanity, despite whatever disagreements they might have, as the disagreements would prove to be insignificant in comparison to the love they had given her throughout her life. All of this happened while she could still hear the television downstairs and some of the conversation her brothers were having.

I see the Archangels often, although they are not the ones whom I connect with on a daily basis. It is hard to put into words the loving presence of my Angelic Friends, whom I have the pleasure to work with. I see them as pure white and gold light overseeing our team of invisible helpers.

There are thousands of Angels of Light assisting humanity; communicating with the masses in the most subtle of ways; making their presence known through our senses, dreams and visions. These highly evolved beings of light give us their love and wisdom, never wanting or asking for anything in return. Their love is unconditional and their wisdom is always an offering.

Our souls have free will and it is up to us if we choose to listen to their advice or not. Their loving truth is administered without judgment or criticism. They only give us what is beneficial and pertinent at that specific moment in time, to aid us on our journey of life.

I have been blessed to have had this divine guidance to help me at key points throughout my life. While receiving their guidance, I have never felt anything besides unconditional love and truth. Although, truth can be hard to hear at times. I found the Angels' gentle way of communicating truth to be astonishing in the way it lacked judgement or critique. As I sit in session with my clients, I feel incredibly blessed and honored to be a part of many wonderful love-filled connections. My heart could explode with the intense feelings of love, joy, and compassion the Angels have for the person before me. These divine communications create deeper connections and awareness of God's loving presence. The Angels' hearts are directly connected to the divine.

Imagine a huge pool of white and gold light. Call it the source of God. See this bright divine light in every Angel's heart, every one of them radiating this magnificent pure light out to all beings. The greatest gift we can give ourselves is to open our hearts and allow ourselves to receive this magnificent pure light. When we allow ourselves to receive the gift of God's love, we can then become conduits of this divine light, thus anchoring the heavenly frequencies into this earthly realm.

Deceased Loved Ones

THE MOST COMMON VISITATION IS THAT OF A DECEASED LOVED one, usually a family member or friend. This type of spirit visits on the wings of love, typically in times of need. They retain some of their earthly persona with the added bonus of offering wisdom and beneficial knowledge from a higher power. Their goals are to protect their loved ones, and bring hope and inspiration, guiding loved ones through challenging times, and encouraging them with their loving presence.

Although all souls are capable of interacting within our realm, when the souls of loved ones visit from the Source of Divine Light, they are in full knowledge and have a deep understanding of what they can and cannot share with us. Too much information may be detrimental to our soul's plan and lessons we are meant to learn. Remember, this earthly plane is comparable to being in school. When our hearts are open with love and compassion, we are learning and growing spiritually every minute of every day. Advice we are given by deceased loved ones is only what is beneficial and relevant at a particular moment in time. Anything more than what is absolutely necessary would not serve us. Whenever I am caught off guard with one of life's curveballs, I often ask my spirit guides: "why didn't I have a heads up on this situation?"

Their response is always: "would it have served you in any way to know about these events beforehand?"

When I look deep inside myself and then outside of myself at the event I am experiencing, my answer to that question is always no.

This has helped me to understand why only certain information is given at the time of a session with my clients. The wisdom shared is always to help clients heal and inspire them with hope, courage, and strength to carry on. I always feel blessed to be a part of such wonderful loving connections. I feel the love that is sent to the person sitting before me. I cannot fully express how this feels. It is so pure and beautiful. My heart bursts with the feelings of unconditional love being expressed.

When the veil, the force that separates the spirit realm from the earthly realm, is thin, interactions with spirits may include the spirit appearing in full form of the physical body the spirit once held. This does not happen often. Our loved ones do not want to scare us. If you are lucky enough to have this experience, it is because they know you can handle it without being frightened. When these loving spirits are present, you may smell floral fragrances, cigar smoke, or mints, among many other odors. Smelling aromas when a loved one is present is just another way of communicating. The smell is usually associated with the person when they lived. Feathers may also appear at your feet and in peculiar places to communicate when loved ones and Angels are nearby. You may hear your name being called or they can communicate telepathically, sending thoughts into your mind, sometimes in the voice you recognize as theirs. Spirits are also capable of physical touch, usually a gentle kiss on the face or a slight tap on the shoulder. A friend of the family experienced a tap on her shoulder while visiting us when no physical presence was beside her, and the rest of us were facing her in conversation. Deceased pets might brush along the side of your leg or create an imprint on the quilt at the bottom of your bed. I have had many messages from my loved ones and Angelic Friends, many in the form of hearts, feathers, coins, and lights flashing on and off. I have also heard loud claps, bangs, and witnessed my phone suddenly talking via the Siri app when I am nowhere near the device. This usually happens when the Angels, loved ones, or clients' loved ones are trying to attract my attention. One such incident happened while I chatted to Vic on the phone. He had just visited a new business location and was asking me if I thought it would be a good fit. He just got the sentence out when right before my eyes I witnessed our television remote control rise with an invisible hand and slam down on the coffee table. Vic exclaimed on the other end of the phone call: "what the hell was that?"

I said: "I guess that is a very firm, yes."

I have witnessed loved ones coming through in times of great need, sometimes highlighting serious health problems. If a loved one can help, they will.

Saving Mary

I HAD TWO WOMEN WHO WERE FRIENDS WITH ONE ANOTHER scheduled for spiritual healing sessions on this particular day. One reading was given to a young woman in her early thirties and the other to a woman in her late fifties. The woman in her fifties, Mary, was so nervous that she was physically shaking. She had never had a spiritual reading before. I sensed that Mary had to be the one to go first. I reassured her and calmed her as I gently guided her to my office, quickly alleviating her fears, and making her feel comfortable. After a short exchange she soon settled down. I proceeded to tune in with my spirit guides. I sensed a deep concern for this lady, it was so intense, I knew her life was in danger. Her late husband suddenly appeared beside her. He told me she had been experiencing dizziness and had nearly passed out at times. He let me know that she had not told anyone. He also gave me the impression her heart was palpitating and she could not catch her breath. I had to deliver the message without frightening her and at the same time stipulate that she needed to seek immediate medical attention.

Cautiously, I told Mary that her loving husband was present and informed her that he had mentioned that she had not been feeling well, having bouts of breathlessness and dizzy spells. She confirmed this to be true. I asked her to promise that she would go to the doctor. She nodded but her husband and the Angels were not convinced she would follow through. I escorted her to the waiting room and beckoned her younger friend into my office. I told her about the messages I had conveyed to Mary. I said, "I am sorry to put this responsibility on your shoulders, but you must take her to the doctor as soon as you leave."

She replied, "is it that serious?"

I heard the Angels say a firm: "Yes!"

I finished the second session and they left. I did not hear anything from either of the two women until a week later. The younger woman called on behalf of Mary's family to explain what had happened. After they left, she called Mary's son and told him what had occurred. Having absolute trust in the message, he phoned their family doctor and made an urgent appointment for his mother. The doctor examined Mary and sent her straight to the hospital's chest clinic. The doctors there diagnosed a pulmonary embolism. The next update came seven weeks later. Mary had been hospitalized during this time and the medical intervention she received allowed her to make a full recovery. The younger woman said the family were eternally grateful. I never heard from or saw Mary again. I was just happy to witness and be a part of a wonderful miracle.

On another occasion, I was in session with one of my regular clients. I asked her about the man named William. She said that was the name of her grandfather. I said, "he said that your dad has been having trouble in the stomach area?" She confirmed this.

I told her: "Your grandpa, William, and my guides are telling you to tell him to go to see the doctor." My guides had highlighted a grey spot in an image of the stomach that looked suspicious and it needed checking out.

When my client gave this message to her dad, he said, "if my dad has made the effort to give me the message, I'm going to make an effort and see my doctor." The doctors found a small cancerous lump. He received medical treatment and was able to make a full recovery.

In one more instance, a mother and daughter visited me every year for a reading. I always looked forward to seeing these lovely people. However, this time, rather than helping save a life, they were helping prepare my client for her transition. The mother came in first and as I was sitting before her, I knew she would not be here the following year. Her loving late husband stood firmly by her side, explaining to me that his wife had a nasty cough that would not subside. She confirmed this was true and I went on to say I could see her and her daughter sitting in the consultant's office looking at her chest x-rays on the screen attached to a wall. "Your husband is telling me to tell you not to be frightened. He will not leave your side," I said. "His loving strength will help guide you."

The daughter came in next. I said to her: "Your dad is telling me to tell you to look after your mum. He knows you've been worried about her and he will support you in the upcoming months." We hugged and said our goodbyes. I was sad to see them go knowing it would be a hard year.

The following year the daughter came to see me alone. She told me that her mother had been diagnosed with terminal lung cancer a few weeks after our visit. Her mother said to her throughout the months, "don't worry, your dad is right by my side and I know he will be the first one to meet me when I leave."

She said, "those words carried her through all of her challenges."

Her mum and dad came through to share a message to her on that day. We both rejoiced in such a loving reunion.

A Mother's Love

My friend, Joanne, and I had known each other since high school. Our boys were good friends and played on the same football team. This meant we would see each other two or three times per week. We also went to yoga class together, which gave Joanne a little relaxation time. She was the mother of four boys and stepmother to two girls. She sure had her hands full. Her home was a happy one and she looked after her large family with love, ease, and grace.

She was six months older which was a constant joke between us. I used to say she would hit each big birthday well before me. She had just turned forty years old when she found a lump in her breast. Everyone advised her to see the doctor, which she did. The doctor did not take her seriously and did not follow up with her. Jo went for a second opinion. Tests were immediately ordered and shortly after she was diagnosed with breast cancer. After a mastectomy, Joanne was given radiotherapy and chemotherapy in the form of a tablet. She recovered from the surgery with an upbeat attitude and a positive outlook on life. This experience motivated her to pursue the hobbies and interests that she loved. We thought it would be a good idea to go deeper into our yoga practice together. We signed up for the six-month British Wheel of Yoga Foundation course which was facilitated by the wonderful yoga instructor we had been seeing regularly for two years. We had a blast. Both being a little mischievous, we would hide out in a corner of the large room, which we dubbed "the naughty corner", and giggle. The yoga class kept both of us sane. It helped Joanne in her pursuit of optimal health and helped me decompress, alleviating the intense pressure I was experiencing and giving me strength to walk through the worst time of my life: months into the course Clair, my stepdaughter, was diagnosed with a brain tumor.

During our last class in the foundation course, we were all asked to meditate while reflecting on a bowl full of pineapple chunks. We had to bring to mind the smell, taste, and feeling of a pineapple and visualize it growing and coming into ripeness for our consumption. We imagined it maturing in the sunshine and saw the fruit with gratitude for the gift of nourishment. After coming back into awareness, we ate the delicious pineapple, said our goodbyes to the other members of the course and our instructor and headed to the car to leave. While walking to the car, Joanne said, "what do you think of *that*?" with a playful smirk on her face.

Still feeling the warmth on my skin from our meditation and walking in the relaxed state of being that I was in as a result of empathizing with the life of a pineapple, without a care or worry in the world, I turned to Joanne and said, "I just want to be a pineapple." We burst into fits of laughter. We told our yoga instructor about this at our next regular session of yoga.

After I moved to California, I received a note from my yoga instructor letting me know that I could now actually be a pineapple, with the sun warming my back and healing all that I had been through.

Joanne battled breast and bone cancer for many years. Her focus was on living with cancer, not dying of cancer. While in California, Jo and I connected over the phone once a week. She and her two youngest boys flew over for a vacation to visit us. Together we took our boys to Disneyland, Universal Studios, and to the ocean for a whale watching tour. I can still picture Joanne scooting around Disneyland on a motorized scooter with a devilish smile on her face and stopping off for cigarette breaks every chance she could. She rolled her own cigarettes and carried a tin of tobacco with her and papers. I will forever treasure these happy memories and all of her quirky habits.

My last physical conversation with Jo was fun and upbeat as always. She had been anxiously waiting for the results from her recent scan. The day we spoke she excitedly shared her good news that the test results had been better than expected. The bone cancer had not spread or grown. I felt a deep relief that my friend was doing well but could not help but sense something was not quite right. I instantly put the thought out of my mind. I did not want to know, but knew in my heart things were not as good as they seemed. Four days later, I received a message from Joanne's older sons asking me to call them as soon as I awoke. My heart sank. I knew it was bad news. They explained that she had developed a bladder infection and had been admitted to hospital. She was sitting up in bed chatting with a friend via text when her kidneys suddenly failed. One minute she had seemed fine and the next she was gone.

The chemo treatment had been long and extensive and her body could no longer cope. I said goodbye, put the phone down, and cried. I knew Joanne was in the light of Unconditional Love. I also knew I would miss my dear friend. A few weeks went by and as I was sitting at my computer feeling sorry for myself, I felt a light touch on the back of my head and heard a familiar giggle. Then, clear as a bell I heard, "Tracey, pull your socks up. You know better." I started to laugh through my tears as I replied, "I'm entitled to grieve, you know!"

"Yes, you are," she said, and then retorted, "I'll give you two minutes to dry your eyes and get back on track, there's work to do! Don't grieve for me, I am well."

I was in no doubt it was my friend. She was concerned for her boys. I had to message them straight away and deliver her love and some important advice. Joanne visits me when there are concerns for her children. She is such a beautiful guiding light.

Grandpa's Guiding Light

GRANDPA'S HEAVENLY VOICE WAS HEARD QUITE OFTEN THROUGHOUT my teen years, starting at the tender age of sixteen. He was constantly and gently guiding me along my journey. Although I had a deep sense of knowing him, I had never actually met him. He had left this physical realm when my mum was a teenager.

It was Saturday night many years ago, when I had gathered with a group of four friends in the car park of the local village public house called the Clarence Hotel. We were not allowed to go inside because we were under the age of eighteen, the legal age limit for alcohol consumption in the UK.

The night air was extremely chilly and our frozen hands and toes needed warming up. My friend was a year older and already had her driver's license. She offered to drive us to a coffee bar located on the outskirts of the village. Everyone eagerly agreed. The thought of wrapping our cold hands around a nice mug of cocoa seemed delightful. We were just about to get into her little yellow two-door car when a young man whom we knew, but not too well, pulled up into the parking lot. He got out and walked over to ask if we would let him join us. My friend's boyfriend said, "of course, follow us." This propelled the other two girls into embarrassing fits of giggles. In an instant, they both turned and started running to my friend's car. The driver and my friend's boyfriend, who claimed the front passenger seat, immediately followed, but for some strange reason I felt bolted to the floor.

I was trying to force my legs to move when I heard a clear heavenly voice in my ear say, "stop, you must get into the other car." I was aghast. *How could I turn around and walk to this young man's car and get in the passenger seat?* I thought. *They'll all laugh at me!* Once again, I heard, "Tracey you must." I knew it was my grandpa. How could I ignore such a strong message? By this time my friend's boyfriend was beckoning me impatiently to get into the remaining spot in the back seat. The words, "I'm going to get in the other car," then flew out of my mouth. Automatically, I walked towards the passenger side of the other car. Amidst the wails of laughter, I got in and buckled my seat belt. My friend's yellow car pulled out of the car park and set off. The young man was so taken aback I had sat in his car that he did not say a word. We set off in pursuit of the yellow car which by this time was out of our sight. The awkward silence broke when he turned to me and asked me why I had chosen to ride with him. Silence returned as I searched some dark corner of my mind for a rational explanation, rather than trying to explain that the Angels and my dead grandpa had urged me to go with him.

When I finally answered him, my mouth opened almost involuntarily and the words, "because that car's going to crash," blurted out. I nearly choked. What the heck had I just said? I sat there numb wondering how I had spoken such words. He did not have time to react, as we turned the hair pin bend, we saw my friend's yellow car had skidded, hit a bollard, and veered off the road, coming to halt in a ditch. With bated breath, we pulled over. Hastily, we unbuckled our seat belts, got out, and ran over to our friends, who had already exited the crashed vehicle. My eyes flitted from one to the next, scanning their ashen faces for any signs of injury. A deep sigh of relief entered my being on the realization that they were just a little shook up. The only place on the car that was badly damaged was the back, left hand side, near the seat allocated to me. If I or anyone else had been sitting there, they would have been badly injured. We did not just have a lucky escape; we were saved by the Angels. On the way home, I silently thanked my guardian Angels and Grandpa while counting my blessings.

Back home, I noticed Mum's face was etched with worry. She said, "I haven't been able to settle all evening. Is everything ok?" She had no idea of the events that had taken place. Mum's intuitive side had alerted her.

That was the first and last time the young man ever joined our group. He was prompted by the Angels to stop that night and help avert a disaster. I doubt that he would have been aware of how important his role was. It must have felt outlandish. Years later, the young man relayed the story word for word to my lovely stepdaughter, Clair. He obviously had never forgotten the incident either.

Divine Mechanical Intervention

IT WAS A COLD, CRISP DAY IN FEBRUARY. VIC AND I HAD BEEN shopping for last minute supplies in preparation for our imminent arrival. We stopped off at a friend's house on the way home. After a wonderful afternoon with our friends, Vic and I said our goodbyes. I waddled out of our friend's home heavily pregnant with Oliver at the time, and eased myself into the passenger seat. I placed the lap belt as comfortably as I could over my huge baby bump. The old Ford Cortina was a golden color with a black roof. Although it was an old car, it was sturdy and had served us well; we had no problems with it up to this point. Vic jumped in and attempted to start the car. The engine sounded sluggish as it turned over. We nervously looked at each other, wondering what could be wrong with the car. After a few more splutters and grinding noises, the engine finally fired up and cautiously we set off. Our friend's home was located on a two-way street, one hundred yards away from a little road bridge. Vic pulled out of the parking spot slowly, taking more care than usual due to the car's new mechanical issues. On any other occasion we would have quickly cruised over the bridge. Only a few feet before we got to the bridge, one of the car wheels suddenly buckled, causing the car to swerve. The bridge was narrow with old stone walls; there would have been no escaping impact had the wheel buckled on the bridge. We both knew our unborn child had been protected by the unexpected delay by engine difficulties from what could have been a serious collision. We took a big sigh of relief and silently thanked our guardian Angels for the divine mechanical intervention.

I seem to be on the receiving end of a lot of activity while in the car. In 1990, on the Easter Sunday that followed Oliver's birth, Vic and I were leaving the home to spend time with relatives, when right at the last-minute Vic picked up the camcorder his dad had loaned us so we could record Oliver's first weeks and brought it with us. He set our old video recorder to record the three-hour long movie "The Ten Commandments". With Oliver safely buckled and all of our baby gear loaded into the car, we left. We spent the day eating, chatting, and having fun. The time passed quickly and, around eight o'clock at night, we headed back home. Both tired from a long day, we sat in the car quietly. As we pulled up at the traffic lights five minutes away from our home, I suddenly heard another voice say, "Tracey, you have been burgled."

I relayed the message to Vic, who received the concerning tip from the Angels calmly and prepared himself to confront the situation. We pulled up outside our home. My heart was pounding with fear. Questions were running through my mind: *Was the intruder still in our home? Was he violent? What should we do?* Vic quietly put the key in the lock and pushed the door open. We noticed the settee had been moved. Vic flicked the light switch and ran to the back door where keys were still swinging in the lock. The thief had quickly run away when he heard us at the front door. He got away with our video recorder, stereo, and other electrical equipment. One thing we were grateful for is that he left a camera filled with precious pictures which was placed on top of Oliver's newly printed birth certificate. At least the thief had a heart. As far as recovering the items stolen from us, we ended up better off than where we had started. Our equipment was old, yet our insurance replaced all of it with new items.

While driving, my mechanical Angel has often directed my attention to possible dangerous situations. I was warned once to drive extremely slow down a street with cars double parked. Then

I heard, "watch out for the child". Within a split second a little one ran out between two parked cars into the middle of the road. If I had not been alerted to take extra caution while driving, the outcome does not bear thinking about.

Apports

THOSE IN THE SPIRIT WORLD CAN AND DO MANIPULATE PHYSICAL objects. The transporting of items from one place to another is commonly known as an apport or apportation. This paranormal transference is not always given the attention it deserves. The rational mind's role of processing information will in most cases cause a person to ignore the amazing body of proof we have been given from our spiritual friends and loved ones that they are with us.

The first one I experienced happened on moving day. We had lived in the Rosedale Close house for six years while the boys were very young. All in all, the energy we had created in that home was a happy one. I had been visited by the deceased previous owner a few times. She was a sweet spirit and only popped in from beyond the veil to revisit her former home on earth.

Many years earlier, when Vic and I were engaged, I had bought him a ring with his initials on it, "VP". This ring had a lot of sentimental value. The ring had been missing for at least five of the years we had lived there. It seemed it had disappeared out of the home, entirely. We had no idea where it was and how it went missing. After many fruitless searches, we never expected to see it again.

The house had been emptied for moving day and I had been left on my own to clean the house from top to bottom for the last couple of hours in preparation for the new owners. I was doing a last-minute check to make sure we had not missed anything or left any belongings behind, when I felt an overwhelming urge to go back into the kitchen. I almost did not go in, my mind kept saying: *you've checked in there twice already.* I ignored my mental chatter and followed the strong nudge from my intuition. Standing in the doorway, I scanned the kitchen. It was clean and empty, as I left it. I was about to close the door when I noticed a glimmer of light reflecting off of something on the counter. I went into the room and to my astonishment, sat on the counter next to the kitchen sink was Vic's ring. I popped it in my pocket as I silently thanked the sweet spirit for bringing it back to us. I smiled to myself as I locked the door and walked away all the while pondering why it was taken and where it could have been.

Sometime later, during a session with one of my more skeptical clients, she asked if her deceased father could give her the ultimate proof of his existence. Her father's spirit had brought to my attention that his wife had his dog tags locked in her safe. He told me he would do his best to bring proof to his daughter. I relayed the message and we parted ways. That evening I received a frantic phone call from her. Breathing heavily and clearly freaked out, she proceeded to explain what had just happened. After leaving our session, she popped into the local grocery store, spent some time shopping, and returned home. As she opened her front door and stepped into the foyer, the lightbulb above her head exploded. She jumped out of her skin wondering what had caused the lightbulb to explode. She went through the hall and turned on the other light. As she looked up at the light fitting where the bulb had blown, she saw something swinging. She fetched her small step ladder, climbed up, and unwound the silver dog tags from the fixture. They were her father's. She called on the phone to her mum and asked where her dad's dog tags were. Her mum assured her that they were in the safe where they have always been. She did not want to upset her mum and kept quiet while gazing at her father's dog tags resting in the palm of her hand. This client asked for the ultimate proof, which she received within a few hours of asking. He did not intend to startle his daughter but probably decided she needed a wow-factor to truly believe.

Another experience of an apportation that I became privy to happened to a young family. A woman had suddenly passed away at the age of thirty-five. She was the mother to three young children who were being cared for by their father, the love of her life. I was asked if I could help bring some peace to this family. I gave a spiritual reading to this sorrowful young man. He was beside himself with grief. As soon as I tuned in, his wife came through loud and clear. She was an incredibly strong soul. She told me the children had accidentally dropped her engagement ring down the outside drain. He confirmed this to be true and explained they had tried to retrieve it to no avail. His wife told me to tell him she was going to bring it back to him as evidence. He asked me how she could do this, which I had no answer for, but I assured him of the message. Three weeks passed when I received a phone call from the young man's sister informing me that the ring had mysteriously turned up on the sideboard in her brother's home. They were blown away by this miraculous happening. This eased the burden of loss and helped the family move forward. A mother's love is incredibly strong and this was one feisty lady. She wanted to make sure her husband was supported so he would be able to embrace the difficult role as a single parent and so that he could take care of their children with the assurance that his wife's soul was still watching over them and helping him in every way possible; thus, easing some of the burden of grief.

The next story happened while I was at a client's home. I was in the conservatory giving individual readings to a small group of women. Halfway through the readings, a young lady in her mid-twenties came in. She sat down opposite to me and I had just managed to ask her name when all of a sudden, our attention was drawn to my car keys placed on the glass coffee table two feet away from us. The keys had been lifted off of the table by an invisible hand, moved a few inches, and then dropped back down. The young lady jumped out of her skin and looked a little ashen. My attention was then drawn to a child in spirit who I

The Silent Apparition

Imprint haunting, a type of apparition, usually provides a glimpse into a past trauma. This type of manifestation, typically human in appearance, gets its name from the fact that there is no interaction with any conscious being. The imprint haunting has a tendency to repeat the same action over and over again. Imagine a group of 18th century British soldiers wearing red coats, bayonets in hand, marching through a wall at a certain time every day, totally oblivious to their surroundings and never communicating with the living. You can liken it to looking through a window in time. I have not had any direct experience with seeing this type of apparition, although I have felt imprinted energy in many locations. There is no rational explanation on how the environment can hold such strong imprints. My spirit guides have taught me that if there is an enormous amount of emotional energy released from a person or many people, especially during deplorable acts of violence, copious amounts of emotions such as fear, anger, sadness and desperation are released from these terrified souls. This profound energetic impact penetrates so deeply it burns layers of imprinted energy into the environment where these atrocities occurred. This pocket of residue energy can feel heavy with rage, sadness, grief and terror. Upon seeing or sensing these strong imprints and emotions and not quite understanding what they are or where they come from, the imagination goes into overdrive and may inadvertently add more feelings and fears, thus strengthening the energy stamp.

There are also positive imprints that can be caused from large happy gatherings, such as music concerts and places where deep love, joy, peace, happiness, excitement, and devotion occur. Albeit, less intense, these positive emotions permeate the atmosphere, creating a gentle energetic stamp. I love going to concert venues and feeling the supercharged energy. It always revitalizes and recharges every cell of my being with the added bonus of watching a favorite artist.

Have you ever sat in a sacred place where others have also previously sat while in prayer and meditation and experienced a deep sense of enlightenment? By sitting in this wonderful space, you may have instantly felt the urge to send love to every realm and every being like those who had come before you. The original intentions and prayers of peace and love created in sacred places have a gentle positive imprint, subtly being felt by all who visit the space. While experiencing these sites, we add our own energy to these wonderful imprints for the next visitor to enjoy, whether we are aware of it or not. It is the feeling and energy that we co-create that lives on as an imprint in this reality long after we have physically left this realm.

This is a testament to the power we hold in our own hearts. If we stood together and consciously focused on emanating love, peace, and joy in the form of golden rays of light that radiate out of our heart centers and connect with each other, we could create such a strong positive imprint. Feelings of lasting love, compassion, responsibility, and wellbeing would be created, inspiring and helping one another and leaving the imprint for future generations to sense and further add to; thus, changing the world.

What can you do when feeling a negative imprint? When encountering an undesirable energy imprint, first and foremost recognize it for what it is and stay calm. You have nothing to fear. Close your eyes and imagine every cell of your being filled with divine white light. Call in the Benevolent Beings to clear the space. Then begin to visualize the golden light of God's Unconditional Love and positive healing energy washing over the dense imprinted energy, dispersing any negativity and transforming it into positive energy. Simultaneously, say a silent prayer asking for Divine Help to heal the cellular memory of the souls affected by the original act of terror and anyone thereafter in the physical and in spirit. This cleansing and healing makes a huge difference as it replaces energy in the space with a peaceful, loving atmosphere, healing the past, present, and the future.

The experience I had in Chichen Itza is a combination of working with imprinted energy, earth healing, and encountering custodians of a sacred space. I never had any thought of visiting Mexico. I never even dreamed of it. The destination seemed so far away and much too expensive. But while meeting my long-time friend, Barbara, for lunch on a warm and bright summer day, the subject of a spiritual mission to Mexico suddenly unfolded. Barbara and I were chatting happily outside a small cafe in Uppermill, a quaint little English village, when out of the blue, Barbara, who is a wonderful intuitive, received a message from her spirit guides. She said, "Tracey, you will be going to Mexico. You have some spiritual work to do there. You will also capture some phenomena on camera." We both started laughing because we could not see how that would be possible.

I stated, "I haven't had any inclination to go to Mexico and I don't even own a camera." After the next bout of laughter died down, we agreed to trust in the message we received. It was just a matter of time until it manifested into physical reality.

Three weeks went by without any mention of the message Barbara conveyed, when Kath, a good friend whom I had worked on for many years in an energy healing capacity, called and said she would like to take me and my family on vacation for Christmas and the New Year. I silently wondered if she was going to say Mexico, when she revealed we would be going to the Dominican Republic. I kept quiet and listened to what she had to say. Without going into further detail, she also mentioned that she was going to go to Mexico in February 2003. I thought perhaps we would not go away in December to the Dominican

Republic, after all. Perhaps she might tag us on to her vacation in February and that was how Barbara's message would manifest. I did not discuss the information I received three weeks prior with this friend. I wanted to wait and see what would happen without my intervention.

Another few weeks went by when Kath called again with an update. She said, "you will never guess where we're all going at Christmas?" I laughed and asked if it was Mexico. She exclaimed, "how the heck did you know?" I told her about the message I received from our mutual friend, Barbara. Directly after the call, I got on the phone to Barbara and let her know the message she had received had started to manifest.

The weeks went by swiftly and we decided to celebrate Christmas early, so the children would not miss out on our family traditions while we were all on vacation. As we sat at the dinner table exchanging gifts, my dear husband, who had no idea what Barbara had said to me about capturing phenomena on camera, passed me this little neatly wrapped box. Inside was a compact camera with a mini video attachment. I looked at him in amazement and explained the second part of Barbara's message. He also gave me Medicine Cards by Jamie Sams and David Carson. I did not realize it at the time, but the oracle cards would be an integrated part of the message. I promptly wrapped and packed my camera and pondered over what my spiritual quest could be.

With an open heart and mind, we headed for the airport to begin our vacation. After ten and a half hours, the plane touched down on Mexican soil. We hastily got our bags and set off en-route to the marvelous five-star hotel my friend had reserved on the oceanfront. Weary after the long plane ride, we retired to bed early. The next morning bright-eyed and bushy tailed, we ate a hearty breakfast and headed out to the beach. While sitting dreamily, looking out at the brilliant turquoise ocean, Kath inquired, "do you know what spiritual work you have to do yet?"

"Nope," I said.

No sooner had the words left my mouth, when I heard my spirit guide say: "Tracey, you must go to Chichen Itza." Chichen Itza is an ancient Mayan city located in the Yucatan Peninsula, famous for its pyramids and ruins.

"I have to go to Chichen Itza," I said, relaying the message I had just heard to the rest of our group.

"That's over two hours away from here!" Kath cried out.

"I have to go. I have this incredibly strong urge from my guides." I trusted the message and my intuition and knew this is where my spiritual journey was heading. Vic did not hesitate to accompany me. The others followed suit.

Three days later we stepped onto a rickety old bus on our way to the ancient Mayan ruins. I could not quell the excitement in my heart. I knew this work was important, although I still was not in full awareness of what I was supposed to do. The bus ride was rather bumpy and hot and humid, but it was no bother to me. I could not help but think how everyone on the bus was blessed, especially while gazing out of the window and seeing so much poverty. I silently prayed the people we passed by would be surrounded by love, joy, healing and prosperity.

We soon arrived at our destination. As we gathered amongst the bustling crowd, a strong sense of recognition surged through me. I knew I had walked this land before. Kath asked what we should see first. I had already noticed a large line forming around Kukulkan, the largest pyramid, and a small entrance before them. "I have to join the line," I asserted with a strong sense of encouragement from my spiritual guides.

As we stood patiently, wondering what it was everyone stood in line for, a lady in front of me suddenly turned around, looked in my eyes, and said, "this is the last time the inner chambers of Chichen Itza will be open to the public. They are closing it the following week for the sake of preservation." The Temple of Kukulkan, also known as El Castillo, is the Mesoamerican step pyramid which houses the Chac Mool in a chamber known as the "Hall of Offerings" and the Red Jaguar in a space understood to be a throne room called the "Chamber of Sacrifices".

In a flash, I knew why I was there and what I had to do. Our turn came to step foot into the narrow passage into the Inner Temple. On entering, I was hit with an intense feeling of being welcomed, helped, and supported by invisible friends. As I climbed the little staircase, I sensed the presence of many people following. If I had not known better, I would have sworn there was a physical crowd behind me. It felt like a beautiful cushion of energy was holding me up and if I leaned back, I would not have fallen—I would have been fully supported by the unseen force that was assisting in healing, cleansing, and releasing the energy of this sacred space. When I reached the top, I looked over my shoulder just to confirm my intuition was correct. Not a single person was there, only a haze of energy like a light mist.

I brought my attention back to the intimate space where both the Chac Mool and the Red Jaguar could be seen. The Red Jaguar is believed to be a throne. Given the composition and detail of the throne and its depiction in other murals, it is also believed by some that whoever was seated on this throne had intended to gain access to *axis mundi,* or point of contact between the heavenly and earthly realms. A mesh grille stood between us and this ancient piece of Mayan history. Kath suddenly felt claustrophobic and left with her husband, Mark, and the children. Vic and I remained, alone in the dark temple with the jaguar figure. Instinctively, I closed my eyes and filled every cell of my being with the light of Unconditional Love and positive healing energy. I visualized the light permeating every part of the Chac Mool, considered to be an altar where sacrificial hearts were placed in ancient times, the Red Jaguar, and the surrounding area of the inner temple. The light held the intentions of cleansing and releasing stagnant energy and replacing it with love, peace, forgiveness, calm, and joy. Flash photography was not allowed. However, Vic remembered that the camera he had bought for Christmas had a video recording feature. He used the camera to record the space while I was performing energy work. When the work was finished, Vic and I turned to descend the staircase when my guides directed us to another part of the site. A voice said, "now you have to go to the cenote with the light of Unconditional Love to bless and transform the oppressive energy held there." Human sacrifice took place at the Cenote Sagrado.

I sat in a quiet spot and did what was requested. I saw many lost souls smile as they moved on to higher realms. I silently thanked our invisible friends for their love, protection, and help. Then, I heard, "the work is now complete."

With the sun glaring down through the dense jungle canopy, Vic and I checked the little camera screen to replay the video, hoping we had caught something, as Barbara had said we would. The video only showed a black screen. We believed that we must not have caught any phenomena. I thought it strange and decided to trust in the message, regardless. We proceeded to enjoy the rest of our vacation with our friends and family in this wonderful part of the world in deep gratitude to our friends for treating us to this remarkable journey. Little did Kath and Mark know, they had been guided by an unseen force and played an important role in this adventure. To them and their kindness of heart, the Angels, custodians of the sacred space, and countless formerly trapped souls are eternally grateful.

Back home in England, with excitement in my heart, I could not wait to share our story. I started to upload the pictures from our trip on the computer. My gaze went to the video clip that Vic and I previously assumed was just a black screen. We did capture something! I clicked the play button on the video and, to my amazement, the jaguar's eye started oscillating light. My spirit guides nudged me to take a still of the video. I did and printed the image out. They then asked me questions about what I could see in the picture. I began to scan the image when right before my eyes the laughing Buddha's face emerged, then King Arthur's crown, a huge eagle, a UFO, and many faces of which I consider to be the guardians of the sacred space. Spirit told me this was a depiction of mankind. I went into a short meditation and was immediately shown a stunning black jaguar with piercing blue eyes. His name was Mula and he was going to walk with me throughout the rest of my life to protect me from any negative energy that might be detrimental to my wellbeing. I came back into this reality relaxed and full of love. I was rubbing my eyes when I heard spirit say, "now unwrap and pick one of the medicine cards Vic bought you."

I placed some cards face down on a table, closed my eyes, and proceeded to pick out a card. I randomly picked Jaguar Medicine. Then I started to read the message:

"Since the death of Skygod, the godlike being who had come from the stars and led the Maya to prosperity and the golden era of spiritual understanding, are the teachings of love, integrity, impeccability, and the power of a compassionate heart had been perverted. The distortion of his Jaguar teachings are degenerated to where the priests were sacrificing human beings, foolishly cutting out the victim's hearts to reclaim the power of the golden days of the Empire. Forgotten was the authentic power of the honourable and loving heart in Skygod's teachings. The Great Jaguar spirit is Skygod's totem."

The Great Jaguar Spirit is Skygod's Totem.

My intuitive friends came to see the video we captured. As we sat in meditation, our dear friend and most beautiful lightworker, Joyce, went into a semi-trance state. She channeled a Mayan energy and gave me a message: "We are most pleased with the energy work you did. The cleansing, healing, and releasing of stagnant energy was a great gift to the earth. In return we are gifting you with the Mayan healing energy to help all." I was completely humbled, still unable to wrap my head around why I was chosen to do this special work. Perhaps it had to do with my birthday, which falls on the spring equinox, a significant astronomical occurrence to many cultures around the world, including the Maya. It is possible that I had unfinished business from a past life, or maybe I had agreed to help before incarnating. I traveled from the UK to Mexico without cost to my family. I am still blown away with the events even though I was a part of it.

After a series of events in my life, I found myself living with my family in Southern California. One day, a lovely lady of Mayan descent came to visit me for a reading. She sat opposite me and gazed into my eyes and suddenly declared, "Tracey you carry the Maya energy!" I proceeded to share my story. She also explained she saw me in a prior life as a child of the night. This revelation confirmed to me the strong sense of recognition I had when I first arrived in Chichen Itza. She described how the ancient Mayans kept a few children inside during the day so they could be taught to read the stars at night. Some time had passed from that meeting and I had not thought much more about the subject until I was browsing the local bookstore and spirit urged me to pick a book up off of the shelf. The book was called <u>Serpent of Light Beyond 2012</u> by Drunvalo Melchizedek. He mentions the earth kundalini (life force energy) which had been located under India, Tibet and Nepal. The kundalini had become stuck and the Maya and many indigenous tribes around the world sat in ceremony to unblock the life force and aid its journey to Chile, Peru, and extending through Mexico and the western United States. This would be completed in the year 2012, and the earth's life force would find its resting place for the next 13,000-year cycle.

Return to the Yucatán Peninsula

IN 2017, LIFE WAS GOING WELL AND MY FAMILY AND I WERE HAPPY and settled in California. Vic worked for an engineering company and I continued to share love, hope, and inspiration through my work as a spiritual intuitive and medium. Every year, Vic and a few colleagues were invited on a four-day builders networking trip that was usually held in a northern state of Mexico called Baja California Sur. Partners were also invited on these trips. The large group usually stayed in the northern part of Mexico, due to its proximity to California. We had a good time on the first trip and were looking forward to the next time we would be in Cabo San Lucas. When the itinerary came through, to our surprise, the group had decided to go to Cancun. Once again, I was being sent to the Yucatan Peninsula without any personal expense. I could not help but wonder what spirit had planned this time.

With implicit trust in my spirit guides, I decided to just go with the flow and see what would transpire, allowing myself to be led every step of the way. I had a strong feeling that I needed to take a crystal infused with love and positive healing energy to plant in one of the ruins at Tulum. I infused the crystal while blessing it with rose oil and sacred sage and tucked it safely away in my travel bag. We arrived at the hotel, after a reasonable flight, to a warm welcome. We had been allocated points to use for various activities or trips. Our friends advised us to book our activities quickly so that we would not miss out on the ones that were higher in demand. Taking their advice, Vic and I breezed over to the agents table and Vic's attention was drawn to the cenotes and caves of the Mayan riviera. I scowled at him and he started to laugh. Swimming is not a strength of mine and the fact we would be underground did not appeal to me at all. Vic and the agent's reassurance won me over, reluctantly. After all, I would be wearing a life jacket. All the while, my mind kept saying: *what the heck are you signing up for?* Once again, I knew I must. I just had to face my fears first.

The day came and off we set. The bus was filled with a nice group of people. I felt safe and comfortable with them. We soon arrived at our destination, filed out of the bus, and stepped onto Mayan land. The instructor passed out our life vests and equipment. We put everything on and proceeded to step into the cool water of the underground cenote. I felt calm and confident while entering and the water was quite soothing. We had only been in the water a few minutes when the light stopped working on my helmet. There were no spare helmets or lights for me to use but we thought it would be ok. I started to swim when, all of a sudden, my life vest came up and over my face and my helmet came down over my eyes. I took in a huge gulp of water and the fear of a thousand lost souls permeated every cell of my being. My heart was pounding so much I thought it would burst through my sternum, swim back to the starting point, and head to the hotel without me. Vic was instantly at my side. With his support I reached the step and regained my composure, reassuring my heart that it would be okay. I knew I had to press forward and would not let this resistance from a negative energy stop me. Vic and I agreed it would be better for me to lie on my back as he pushed and guided me through the deep parts of the water. The energy of fear I previously felt was replaced with laughter at my predicament. Sharing this humorous moment with Vic instantly raised the vibration of the space from one of fear to one of lightheartedness.

I was not in any position to take pictures and as a group we only had one waterproof pouch between us. A member of our party was a beautiful and caring young lady and she had kindly agreed to take the pictures and send them to us later. Surprisingly,

I was quite relaxed as we moved further underground. I then felt the presence of many guardians bringing their love and help from beyond the veil, once again bringing the light of Unconditional Love and positive healing energy to the area we swam in and the surrounding caves. I knew some phenomenon would be caught on camera, I was just not sure what. Later that day, the images were sent to our group via the messenger app, and I noticed one containing a heart image in the wall and one containing the image of the guardian of the space.

A few days later we set off to Tulum, another great Mayan city. We followed the tour guide around the many ruins, listening intently. I had the tiny crystal in the palm of my hand the whole time, waiting for the right moment to plant it. I passed the stone on to Vic to hold and bless and in an instant, he was bit by a bug. He slapped his leg and a little blood got on his fingers and transferred to the crystal. I joked that perhaps we needed a blood offering. He gave me a sideways glare as he was being bitten repeatedly. Shortly after we separated from the group, Vic noticed a secluded little spot of ruins that were not cordoned off. He voiced that it must be the place we were meant to go. We sat on this small wall, blessed the crystal once more and placed it in the ruins. This would aid in the cleansing and healing of the land. Another job done. The next day we flew back home.

On our return, I excitedly looked through the pictures, finding out that much more phenomena had been captured in the photos. Barbara's message to me from more than a decade prior had been fulfilled for a second time. I am not sure if I will ever return to the Yucatán Peninsula. I suppose it depends what else my soul agreed to do. Although, while writing this I heard clearly, "you will."

Living Spirits

LIVING SPIRITS ARE INCREDIBLY RARE METAPHYSICAL OCCURRENCES. They happen when one encounters the spirit of a person who is still alive, but is physically at another location. This is mind boggling to experience. These living spirits usually appear via some sort of teleportation, brought on by a strong need to be somewhere out of a deep concern for a loved one. Such manifestations are unexpected, to say the least, and the person teleporting is not usually mentally aware of what they have done, although the soul-self is in full knowledge and control. I have only experienced this phenomenon when the living spirit is either unconscious, suffering from diseases such as Alzheimer's or dementia, or when they are preparing to leave the physical body and return to the light of Unconditional Love.

My introduction to such an event happened in my early thirties. I had been asked to do spiritual readings for a group of people in a neighboring town. After a forty-minute drive through the green English countryside, I reached my destination. I was always curious to see what would unfold during these types of gatherings and what kind of information or wisdom the Angels would surprise me with. Although I was unfamiliar with the people I was headed to meet, I had total trust in the Angels that the evening would bring about the highest good for those who were attending. I was greeted at the door by the woman that had arranged the gathering, whom I had never met in person and had up to this point only spoken with briefly on the phone. She guided me to a room adjacent to the living room, where I settled onto a chair and waited for her to bring in her first guest for a reading. I proceeded to give one-to-one thirty-minute readings to a small group of ladies. The next guest entered the small room and sat down before me. I was about to start delivering messages that I was receiving from my guides and the angels for the middle-aged lady in front of me, when another spirit interjected.

The spirit said, "my name is Elizabeth and this is my daughter. I have severe health problems and I am here to tell her not to worry about me anymore. I will be more than fine." I became confused by the message, thinking her mum had recently passed. Her daughter told me that she had just arrived from the hospital, which was five minutes away, to see me in the hope she would receive a message about her mum. We both got a big surprise from the spirit of her mother delivering a direct message while her physical body was resting in a hospital bed in a coma. This message brought an incredible amount of serenity to her loved ones. As the matriarch of their family, she wanted to reassure them before she made her peaceful transition, which came in the early hours of the next morning.

In another encounter with a living spirit, I again was meeting a client for the first time. The spirit of this client's father-in-law attracted my attention. He told me that his family had a big decision to make regarding his wellbeing. He said he was on a life support machine, and it was okay for the family to let him go. He said he would not be coming back. As I spoke his message aloud, my client and I both looked at each other teary-eyed. I asked her if the message resonated with her. She confirmed this to be true. She explained that her husband and his family had an appointment with her father-in-law's doctor that very afternoon to talk about removing this courageous spirit's life support.

I have also had a deeply personal experience with a living spirit. My dear friend and mentor, Joyce, had unfortunately succumbed to Alzheimer's. While in the physical, Joyce Alsop was an amazing lightworker and an outstandingly gifted healer for over sixty years. She was also quite eccentric. Her heart would burst with love and compassion for all and she was not afraid to express these feelings. She was eloquent with her words and was a wonderful philosopher. I could not understand why she stayed in her physical body, enduring her circumstances of disease for so long, while she had such a detailed understanding of the esoteric and the freedom that awaited her soul. This misunderstanding continued until her spirit came to me and exclaimed that she needed to stay anchored by her physical body in this physical realm so she could be as close as possible to others in order to bring about healing and love on this plane of duality. She said her physical body would pass when she had completed her work, which at the time of the message would not be for a couple of years.

I was able to see her one last time before she transitioned into the light of Unconditional Love. It was during this meeting that I was able to witness yet another miracle. Before taking me to see our friend, Barbara and Jean informed me that Joyce, who was in her early nineties, had not been lucid for quite some time. They explained that I should not expect Joyce to have any recognition or knowing of who I was. Joyce was also severely hearing impaired and communication would be difficult. Essentially, I was going with the purpose of saying goodbye. We arrived at the care home and found Joyce in the small eating area with her shoulders slumped forward and her head bowed. I pulled a chair up in front of her and said, "hi, Joy-cee." I grabbed a hold of her hand. She lifted her head and I gazed into her eyes. I watched tears well up in her eyes as she recognized me. We had a conversation about how I had come back from California on a holiday and was there to visit her. We talked about how she was feeling. At this point, Jean began to video record our conversation. While speaking to Joyce, I was projecting the energy of the words I was saying. A fluid stream of light consciousness traveled between us. She understood and answered all of my questions, to the shock of Barbara and Jean, who were moved to tears. We then escorted Joyce to her room to grab her coat and while we helped Joyce put her coat on,

Jean and Barbara pointed out that Joyce did not have her hearing aids in throughout our exchange. They were perplexed.

Joyce was able to join us for an outing to the garden center up the road from the care facility, where I was able to fill her in on all of the adventures I had experienced in California. Jean drove us all back to the care home. As we said our goodbyes, I held Joyce in a tight embrace. She pulled away from me and said, "I won't see you again, will I?" We never did see each other again in this physical reality. Although the four of us shared an understanding and a belief in the afterlife, the sadness and pain of losing our friend and mentor still weighed heavily on us as it does anyone.

In this meeting, Joyce's soul did the opposite of what she had done when she shared her message with me as a living spirit. Her soul was able to override the deterioration of her mental mind and reclaim her body, even bypassing her hearing disability for a short period while she spent the day with us. She had done what should have been deemed impossible and we were able to witness the sheer strength of her incredible soul.

A different type of living spirit, astral projection, is the act of the spirit leaving the body for a short time and going on a trip to different dimensions or other places on the earthly plane. Those who are skilled in astral projection have the ability to control their soul and temporarily separate it from their body, deciding when and where they will travel. Others have experiences of leaving the body during a traumatic incident. Some have reported observing their bodies from above being worked on by emergency responders, doctors, and nurses. These souls stay connected to their physical bodies via a metaphysical gold and silver cord which is impossible to break unless it is our time to pass over. Astral travel is a wonderful experience proving the soul is separate from the physical body and continues to live after the body has died.

I leave my body while sleeping and do rescue work for lost souls to help them move on to the light of Unconditional Love. I have also been known to comfort the living, having had many clients and friends tell me they have been visited by my spirit during the night in their time of need, bringing calmness, reassurance, and comfort. I have never consciously left my body while awake. I prefer to stay in the physical body during waking hours. However, I have been told by many people that my soul has physically presented itself to others during the day, as if I was standing right in front of them. This is usually when they are afraid. This type of phenomena is sometimes attributed to the Sadhus, the holy men and women of India, who believed they could consciously manipulate time and space, giving them the ability to simultaneously be in different locations.

There are other, less socially acceptable ways which may lead to an out-of-body experience, but these are not advised. In his younger years, Vic and a couple of his friends had been relaxing and listening to music while smoking a joint of marijuana. Vic, in a relaxed state, left his body and floated towards the door. His friend from across the room, seeing Vic's spirit, pointed and yelled, "now! Back in your body!" Instantly, Vic was back in his physical form. Vic did not intentionally leave his body, but his experience was confirmed for him by his friend's "seeing".

Orbs and Other Manifestations of Spiritual Energy

AN ORB IS A BALL OF LIGHT THAT APPEARS TO THE NAKED EYE OR unexpectedly in a photo or video. They appear in a variety of colors, but more often than not are white or blue. One or more may appear in an otherwise normal photograph when the photo is taken in an area of strong psychic energy. These areas are often distinguished by unexplainable density in the atmosphere and a feeling of heightened awareness that there are many beings around without seeing them. Some people also experience a chill in the air or goosebumps on their skin in these places. In my experience, orbs are the physical materializations of spiritual energy. It is easier for a nonphysical soul to manifest these primitive forms than it is to create a full-body apparition, which also runs the risk of frightening the human observing them. These wonderful balls of light are being shown to us as visual evidence of the metaphysical. When captured on video, you may often see an intelligence behind the orb's movement. You may see that it is directed and controlled by the spirit from which it emanates. Perhaps this is the whole idea orchestrated by highly evolved beings of light (Angels) to bring more awareness into our physical reality of their existence in the hopes that humanity realizes there is a higher power and other dimensions, thus inspiring them to take responsibility for their actions and to grow spiritually.

When the Angels are present, I see many little colored star lights blinking on and off in the room. It is quite a magical light show. Witnessing such activity right before my eyes always makes me smile and brings joy to my heart. Other times, I see physical energy manifestations as silver or golden squiggles moving across the room. These are always connected to highly evolved beings. Feelings of unconditional love fill every corner of the space when these star lights and squiggles are present. On some occasions the whole room changes in color and light, usually to a pink, white, gold, or green glow.

More than two decades ago, I was in a meditation group that met every few months to send prayers and healing light out to the world. Joyce, Barbara, and I would make the hour-long journey to the home of our friend, Jean, who resided in a different town. I was the youngest person in this group and felt honored to be included with these women that shared a wealth of knowledge and years of experience dealing with the metaphysical. Arriving at Jean's house, we exchanged pleasantries and warm hugs and headed down into the room Jean designated for us to work in. I could feel the excitement and warmth in the atmosphere as we descended the old steep staircase. Jean had meticulously prepared the space we would be sitting in, which we lovingly referred to as "the cellar". At the bottom of the stairs, we removed our shoes and allowed Jean to cleanse our auras with white sage and the old eagle feather she had been given by a dear Native American friend, Jerome. Jerome had adopted Jean into his family and affectionately named her "Yellow-Hair" while she lived with him on the reservation in Oklahoma during her travels away from the UK.

I was not expecting anything out of the ordinary, as ironic as that seems, but *wow!* I received a huge surprise. We sat in a circle with just a candle to bring a small amount of light. Joyce opened with a prayer and an intention to call in all of the Angels and benevolent beings of light and our spirit guides to assist and protect us. Then we proceeded to enter a deep meditative state. While in meditation, my guides gently whispered in my ear: "Tracey, come into awareness and open your eyes." I did as I was asked and was amazed to see with my physical eyes that a large field of light made of many colors slowly moving and vibrating towards me from out of the darkness; and as it did, it filled the whole room. As the magnificent field of energy approached me, consuming the space with its sheer size and movement, I could feel myself shrinking so much that I felt two-inches tall in the presence of such glorious light of purity and love. I instantly felt the Holy Spirit was present to reassure us of the divine and loving existence of the Higher Power. The energy was so overwhelming I felt I should be on my knees before it to receive its blessing for all of earth kind; not out of fear, but out of complete awe. At the same time, I felt I was within it, engulfed by the limitless energy that had manifested before us. This energy that we had become a part of was sent out to every part of the world to bring love, peace, and healing wherever needed.

While that experience with the manifested spiritual energy continues to stand out most to me, two other amazing manifestations of orbs that I have witnessed happened recently, within a few months of each other, and with other witnesses involved. The first of the two appeared while I was halfway through a reading with a young woman. Out of the corner of my eye, I saw a huge golden-yellow dome-shaped light appear over the door in my office. Within an instant of attracting our attention, the light exploded, raining down sparkles of light. The young lady before me stared wide-eyed. I asked if she had seen what I had seen. Startled, she confirmed that she had also seen the golden exploding orb. The second manifestation took place while I was in session with a couple, a young man and his wife. The golden orb lit up over and just behind his wife's head. Both husband and wife witnessed the light emanating from this orb, which was now shining light directly onto her. Instead of disappearing, the orb this time moved across the room and stopped on the wall behind me. The young man let me know that the orb remained there for the rest of the reading. In both sessions we had received beautiful bright blessings from the Angels.

For years I have been trying to capture the images of genuine orbs as I see them in real-time. Any time I would ready my phone or camera, they would evade me. In 2020, however, I experienced an explosion of visual activity and was able to capture most of it via digital media forms, including the security camera on Vic's steel shop floor, and on my phone during a return trip to Sedona, Arizona. It is important to be discerning when observing what might appear to be orb phenomena. How are real orb pictures distinguished from false ones? Some light shapes appearing in photographs and videos may just be flashes reflecting off of small insects or airborne dust particles. Other light shapes appearing may be lens flares, which happens when light comes into the camera lens that is not part of the image being captured. These reflections can produce spectacular circular orbs on the photographs; however, these are not true orbs. Rule out these false orbs and look at what you are left with.

Full Body Manifestation

THIS VISITATION IS QUITE RARE. THE SPIRIT APPEARS IN SOLID form. One may not even be aware they have encountered a spirit. One cold fresh December morning I was walking up the path to Oliver's school when I noticed an acquaintance walking with her child and a male figure close by her side. He had a large smile on his face. He was short in stature, his hair was dark and wavy, and he wore a white cotton shirt with rolled up sleeves. There was something quite odd about him. I could not put my finger on it or understand why he only had a shirt on in the middle of December. When I reached the gated entrance to the school playground, I turned to open the forest green colored bolted gate and entered into the school yard. I turned around, expecting to see my friend with her child and the male figure. The male figure was no longer with them. I asked her where her male friend was. She looked at me with a puzzled expression on her face. She said, "Tracey, there were only the two of us." I shook my head and smiled to myself, all the while wondering why this spirit showed himself to me.

My Angelic Friends explained that it was a lesson in seeing. This gentle way of seeing a full apparition has happened on quite a number of occasions. I call them undercover Angels. I have seen many in the guise of homeless people. Perhaps spirits take this form to see how we behave with people who some consider lesser human beings due to their circumstances? There is no such thing as a lesser human being. Other disguised Angels appear in times of need. They show up to help and then disappear again. I always get a sense that something feels a little odd, not in a bad way, just not quite normal. It all makes sense after the Angel in disguise suddenly disappears.

This second story involves a full body manifestation of a soul that had come to help her loved one, after he experienced a traumatic death and for a small moment in time had not realized he had died. In November of 1968, Barbara, her husband, Tony, and their beautiful baby boy of six months slept peacefully at home. Barbara was suddenly jolted awake. She bolted upright and before her eyes in the bedroom chair was the clear apparition of an older lady dressed in old fashioned attire. She wore a long, dull, grey skirt and draped over her head and shoulders was a woolen fawn colored shawl. Alarmed, Barbara asked "who are you? What do you want?"

Telepathically, the mysterious intruder said, "I have come for him."

Barbara intuitively knew she meant Tony, her husband of two years. Barbara replied, "you cannot have him!" She then got back under the covers, wrapped her arms tightly around Tony, and fell into a deep sleep.

When she woke the following morning, the incident had left her mind, no worry, stress or anxieties whatsoever. She felt calm and in control. Her mental mind did not understand why she had no concerns after this alarming encounter. Her intuitive side had been strong throughout her life, so she put this down to just another strange occurrence.

Tony went out Friday night that same week, as usual, for a pint of beer and a catch-up with his friends. As the evening progressed, Barbara became increasingly worried. Tony was out later than normal, and she began to feel uneasy. Tony was not much of a drinker. He worked early on Saturday mornings and would not stay out late on Friday nights. At 11:30 PM, Barbara heard her baby let out a piercing scream and quickly ran upstairs to soothe her child. When she got to the bedroom, she found her baby fast asleep. Looking over her sleeping child, wondering what could have caused him to let out such a cry, she heard the front door open and close. Feelings of relief swept over her as she made her way to the top of the steep stairs to ask Tony why he had stayed out so late. Her heart started to pound, her mouth became dry, and no words were spoken as she gazed down the stairway to the empty foyer. A shiver of fear and knowing ran down her spine. She slowly made her way downstairs, holding back the tears welling in her eyes. A few moments later, a loud rap on the door knocker sent shock waves throughout her home. Filled with fear, Barbara opened the door and was met with two uniformed police officers. She took them through to the living room. They asked her to sit down. Everything was a blur as they proceeded to gently tell Barbara that Tony had been in a terrible accident in which he had been hit by a vehicle while crossing the road.

In the background, blurring out from the police officer's walkie-talkie, Barbara heard, "He didn't make it. He's dead."

Barbara felt her world crumbling all around her in shock and disbelief. She did not know what to do. She sensed something was being omitted, and the story she had been led to believe about Tony's accident was not entirely true. Tony had multiple broken bones and severe trauma to his liver and spleen. He passed away at the side of the road. At first his soul, in so much shock, had not realized he had died and continued to make the journey home to his beautiful wife and adorable baby boy.

Weeks later, Tony's family told Barbara that his ninety-two-year-old grandad had been heartbroken by the news of his grandson's passing. His words were, "why didn't God take me instead of my twenty-three-year-old grandson?" They asked her if she would visit him and take the photos they had just had developed of Tony with his Grandad, Dad, and baby, four generations proudly standing together.

The following weekend, Barbara tucked up her baby snuggly in the pram and set out on the forty-five-minute walk to Tony's grandad's house. His grandad was so happy to see them. He made

Barbara a cup of milky tea and offered her shortbread biscuits. He was in awe of his great-grandson and after reminiscing, Barbara proceeded to give him the newly developed photos. He gazed over them teary eyed, then promptly got up and walked over to his old weathered sideboard. He reached in and pulled out a small cardboard box full of old photos. He passed some pictures over to Barbara. As she gazed over them, she saw the familiar person sitting in an open top horse drawn carriage. The woman she recognized was wrapped in a woolen shawl she had seen only days before. She asked Tony's grandad who the lady was. He looked at the photo and with a smile on his face, replied "that's my wife, Tony's grandma." Tony's grandma had passed many years before. Tony and his family had never mentioned anything about his grandma to Barbara. On this revelation, Barbara knew that Tony was in safe hands; his loving grandma had come with the light of Unconditional Love to help him make the transition from this realm to the next. Barbara said this was the one thing that helped her during this horrific time, filling her with a deep sense of peace and giving her the strength and courage that she needed to continue on her life's path.

The official story of Tony's accident is that he had been hit by an unmarked police car being driven by a plain clothes detective at high speed in pursuit of a red Mini Cooper. Barbara heard rumors and wondered if the rumors were based in truth. Folks around town were saying that they had witnessed the same detective drinking for some time in a local bar that evening. No more information or evidence about the red Mini Cooper allegedly being pursued ever came to light. A blanket of silence fell over the police department, protecting the driver's name and avoiding bad publicity. The inquest ruled the driver was only forty percent to blame and Tony was largely at fault for crossing the road while being intoxicated. In Barbara's time with Tony, he had never arrived home drunk. The likelihood that he had been intoxicated enough in this instance to walk into an unmarked police car in high-speed pursuit of a red Mini Cooper was slim-to-none. Barbara sensed she was not being given the full facts. The feeling of helplessness was incredibly frustrating for all who knew and loved Tony.

The truth is the truth and always comes to light, but not necessarily in this reality. Everything done, good, bad, or indifferent is recorded. This is known as the universal law of karma. You may be familiar with the saying, "what goes around comes around".

All of our lives, past, present, and future are and will be stored in the Great Hall of Knowledge, also known as the Akashic Records. The Earth Plane is a school of duality. We can either stay on the path of light, working hard to clear past karmic actions by our good deeds or we can walk in the shadows, never learning nor growing. The choice is ours. Let your heart be your moral compass; it will always guide you to do the right thing. The philosophy of the heart being the true source of the mind and intuition can be traced back in the Zang-Fu Theory of Oriental Medicine. In this school of thought, the heart "houses" the mind, or *shen*, which is more closely compared to the spirit or soul. When one is guided by the heart, they are more closely aligned with their truest essence. Apart from a small minority, the rest of us on earth have not learned all of our lessons. If we had, we would not have come back. We are here to wipe out our karmic debts while being guided by the love of a higher power throughout our lives so as not to add to that debt.

There are many finer points regarding karma. One important point I should mention is intention. We have all made mistakes and done and said things that we regret during our lives. The Angels told me that bad karma is only amassed if there is an intention to cause harm. When our intentions are honorable, even when things do not work out in the best of ways, we receive grace for good intentions. If another person chooses to interpret our words or actions in a negative way, bad karma is still not accumulated, as we are not responsible for another person's perspective or feelings. My guides always tell me to make sure my intentions are good in everything I do. It is that simple. Living in this way offers the answer to eliminating karmic debt and breaking the karmic cycle. Once you have cleared and not incurred any more karma, your soul will not have to reincarnate on the earth plane again. They went on to say, "you all have off days, but even so you must not waste your time seeking revenge or wishing someone ill," as nothing escapes universal law. The Angels have pointed out that one step towards spiritual growth and breaking the cycle of karma is understanding what it was from within which has been triggered to elicit an unsympathetic response. What is it that has irritated or upset you? Trace it back to the point of past pain and use the exercise on Healing the Cellular Memory, which appears in a later chapter of this book. This can help release feelings of anger, inadequacy, frustration, and sadness. It can be difficult to fight the temptation to react in an adverse manner when hostile circumstances or antagonistic actions appear in life.

I have found that by remaining neutral and nonreactive, everything passes swiftly with more ease and grace, because it becomes easier to gain clarity on how to best deal with the issue at hand. However, this does not apply in situations of danger and abuse, or in other situations where immediate action needs to take place for the safety of self and others. Barbara forgave the actions of the driver knowing in her heart and mind he never intended to harm her husband. She had more difficulty coming to terms with the injustice of having Tony's memory tarnished when the police department portrayed him as a drunken, incoherent man for the sake of covering up another's actions. If they would have approached the situation with honesty and integrity, by apologizing for their part, it would have been a lot easier for Tony's family and friends to make peace with the incident. Barbara and I feel sorry for the driver, who held this terrible burden in his heart for over fifty years. It must have caused a considerable amount of guilt. If only he would have been allowed to talk to Barbara. I might add: Tony's souls would have forgiven everyone as soon as he was in the light of Unconditional Love.

Barbara and Tony's friend, Cliff, came to Barbara's rescue, helping her in many ways after the loss of her beloved Tony. Over a few years, their friendship became stronger and stronger, love blossomed between the two, and Cliff and Barbara married.

Cliff was a wonderful husband, father, and grandfather. He was always willing to help anyone in need and was loved by all. After a brave battle against vascular dementia, Cliff made his transition home to the light of Unconditional Love. I was shown his transition by the angels. Amongst his loved ones waiting to greet him stood his dear friend, Tony. Surrounded by the light of love, they embraced. Tony thanked Cliff for looking after Barbara and the boys, their son and grandsons, as they walked arm in arm into the light.

Within twenty-four hours of passing, Cliff sent me a message from beyond the veil.

A Letter to My Beautiful Wife:

My mind wasn't very strong and there was confusion in my heart.
We couldn't be physically together when I left this earthly realm;
I saw you a few days before, in my mind's eye—
the love I felt filled my heart and soul;
You wrapped me in the golden light of unconditional love and with your reassurances I knew it was safe to go.
My loved ones held my hand and guided me to the Angel's light.
Our love is eternal. I wanted you to know:
My light shines brightly guiding you as you go.

All my love, Cliff.

This meant so much to Barbara. She had not been able to visit Cliff for the five weeks prior due to the many restrictions created during Covid-19. The day before Cliff transitioned, four of us energetically connected to send love, healing, and reassurance to Cliff so he would know it was safe for him to leave his body. This light that we helped to create guided him on his path home towards the light of Unconditional Love. While this took place, Barbara saw in her mind's eye Cliff's soul leaving his body and as he left, he blew her a kiss and said, "thank you".

A few months later, Barbara, along with her niece and nephew, went to the garden center to buy a lilac tree to plant in Cliff's memory. When she got there, she noticed a beautiful yellow rose and instantly felt drawn to buying it. Her niece followed her lead. They popped the two plants into their cart and enquired about a lilac tree. They did not have any in stock and she agreed to pick one up the following week. Later that day, Barbara had just finished planting the love-filled bright yellow rose bush in a pot when the phone rang. It was her niece, who was incredibly excited. She asked Barbara if she had read the label with the name of the rose they had just purchased. Barbara realized that she had not. She went to the pot, turned over the tag hanging from the plant, and read the name: "50th Anniversary Rose". The surprise brought tears to her eyes. Barbara and Cliff were approaching their fiftieth wedding anniversary when he passed. Love is eternal, there is no distance between souls that carry the energy of love, and messages and gifts can come from beyond the veil in many different ways.

Spirit Guides

IN MY LATE TWENTIES, THE FREQUENCY OF METAPHYSICAL EVENTS and spiritual experiences in my life exploded and propelled me on the path as a spiritual healer and medium. In today's terms, I am known as a conscious channel, someone who consciously receives and communicates messages from the spirit realm. As soon as I tune in for a reading or healing session, I am engulfed in the healing light of Unconditional Love, peace, and calm. This transformation into an intuitive state of being allows me to convey the magnificent light and wealth of information coming from the metaphysical dimensions to my clients. As a result of decades of practice, I am now able to energetically shift into the state of consciousness needed to converse with spirits, instantly. In the majority of sessions, I feel I am meeting with old friends even though I might not have met them in this lifetime. When I am in session with clients, I am aware and conscious of everything that is being said, while receiving, sensing, and hearing messages from the divine light of the Angels, spirit guides, and loved ones. I always consider myself blessed to be a physical facilitator. As a member of a team of such benevolent beings of light, I witness so many miraculous happenings and connections. This often serves to deepen my own faith, wisdom, and understanding, enhancing and aiding my own spiritual journey towards enlightenment.

For the first few years after awakening, I had daily counseling sessions from my spirit guides. They shared their wisdom and offered their understanding of the purpose of my life. They gave insight on the lessons I was learning at specific moments. I consider each one of my guides a gift. I have deep gratitude for the feelings of heart-centered knowingness that I experienced when facing adversity and acquired a deeper spiritual understanding, empathy, compassion, strength, unconditional love, and so much more. My experiences have inspired the creation of tools to help others in the best way possible in their time of need.

Prior to my awakening, I heard my guardian Angel and my grandad frequently during my childhood and adolescence. These were not daily occurrences, but the loving voices whispering in my ear tended to be clear and strong when I needed divine guidance, hope or protection. Their guiding light alleviated much of the chaos that infiltrated my turbulent childhood. In my early days, connecting with my spirit guides was a blast. They came through crystal clear, showing themselves in physical form with the identity they carried forward from their previous incarnation. My guides told me who they were and how they intended to assist humanity and this earthly realm. Each one had selflessly come to help raise the vibration in this plane of duality. I felt blessed to be part of a team of extraordinary souls in service to humanity and in their quest to raise consciousness. As time went by and my spiritual awareness and knowledge grew, I did not need to see my spirit friends as individuals anymore. They eventually merged into one conscious energy of glorious divine light. I recognize each bright light's soul-identity. This is just a knowing of who is who. I have always struggled to explain this phenomenon.

When I first awakened, I needed the mental construct of a physical connection to allow my mind to conceptualize this huge awakening I was experiencing. It had such an impact on my life. Everything had to be unveiled at exactly the right moment in time, otherwise I would not have been able to cope with all of the information. As the weeks, months, and years flew by and with many daily teachings, I realized that the soul is so much more than a prior identity. I began to see each spirit as a magnificent being and a part of the light of God's perfection, and no longer needing my hand held in this regard. I had learned we are all elements of luminescence, low temperature emissions of light, working as one bright light with the guidance and supervision of The Angels. Every now and again I do see my old friends' faces smiling at me in a haze of white light. Perhaps it's a little gift of remembrance. Reminiscing on the prior identities of my guides always warms my heart and makes me smile, taking me back to the time when they first introduced themselves.

Looking back at the amazing connection and wonderful validations and experiences I have had with a few of my spirit guides—although I do honor, love, and cherish all of the wonderful teachers from spirit I have had the pleasure and honor to work with—I am in deep gratitude to these particularly beautiful souls for their patience, love, wisdom, and light.

Let me start at the beginning.

My spiritual explosion began one weekend when I had decided to sign up for an energy healing workshop at our local metaphysical store, The Crystal Cave. I was nervous, and being painfully shy, I asked Mum to come along for moral support. The little shop was filled with crystals and many more delightful offerings. We entered the space reserved for the workshop and took our seats amongst the circle of strange faces. The facilitator went through the introductions and formalities. We then proceeded to practice quietening our thoughts and deep breathing in preparation for a guided meditation. I quieted my mind and felt at one as I was taken deeper and deeper into the meditation. This was the first time I had ever meditated. I felt the warmth of the energy surrounding, loving, and protecting me. Our instructor taught us about different energies, frequencies, and techniques by using various exercises. To better understand energy, we learned how to feel it by creating the intention of holding energetic spheres in the palms of our hands. Working with this energy ball, we expanded the condensed vibration of energy into huge spheres of tingling warmth. Progressing from that exercise, we went on to detect each other's energy field and to scan the body with our hands to find cool spots, places where the energy was depleted and needed a boost of healing light. I was amazed by what I was feeling and experiencing. Even though I had been intuitive all my life, I never understood its significance or what relevance it would have to my life's purpose.

The next exercise involved different colored fabrics. The point of this exercise was to see which color one's aura needed in order to become healed and balanced. It did not quite work out that way for me. While I was sitting blindfolded, Mum began placing a fabric patch of color on my back. In my mind's eye I instantly saw yellow and told her. She proceeded to place various colored patches in the same spot and each time I "saw" and spoke the correct color. This had created quite a stir and unbeknown to me, everyone had gathered around to watch. The ninth piece of cloth I sensed was navy blue, once again this was correct. They declared there was one last color to place on my back. I saw navy blue again which was confusing. I said, "it feels like navy blue again, but you've just done that one so it must be black." They removed my blindfold and I looked around at the smiling faces as the facilitators held up the navy-blue cloth. They had placed it on my back a second time. This was a lesson to trust in my intuition rather than try to rationalize perceptions with my mental mind. After this experience, I began to practice energy healing on family and friends. Through daily meditation and prayer my guides started to reveal and introduce themselves in preparation for the spiritual wisdom they had to share.

I have encountered many types of spirit guides throughout my life. They come and go depending on levels of growth and need at certain moments in time, assisting all with their area of expertise. Some of my guides, when in their prior physical forms, had been doctors, mechanics, artists, energy healers, veterinarians, wisdom speakers, and nurses, to name a few. They came to assist humanity, the earth, and all creatures in this realm. They help by inspiring, encouraging, and gently guiding us on our paths.

While interacting with the guides of others, I am exposed time and time again to the love they hold for their ward. This was true of the guide I met when Victoria asked me to accompany her to one of my grandson's cardiology appointments. As we were speaking to the cardiologist, who was taking great care and consideration when explaining the prognosis for my grandson's condition to us, I heard, "he's good, isn't he?" Beaming with pride, the cardiologist's spirit guide felt the need to express his feelings of admiration for the cardiologist, while also assuring me that my grandson was in great hands.

You should always feel a deep sense of love and knowing when connecting with a spirit guide. Although, what we might perceive as a new spirit guide is actually an old friend. In the grand scheme of things, we know them and have agreed to connect at a specific time before reincarnating. The guides closest to us are our beautiful soul family from the other side. One in particular has been assigned and agreed upon to guide us from the moment we leave the spiritual realm. Most of us refer to this guide as a guardian Angel. We know we can trust them implicitly. Even though we have no recollection of them due to an amnesia pill, metaphorically speaking. This happens before entering this earthly realm—our spirit companion knows all aspects of our life lessons and goals. Their job is to share wisdom and encouragement and to protect us while we navigate our way through life's many twists and turns.

Our spirit guides have lived many lives in which they learned empathy and understanding and because of this they are able to view our quests with objectivity and nonjudgement. They champion us and gently remind us to be the best version of ourselves by tapping into the deep knowledge we carry in our subconscious memory. They communicate to us in many ways, typically via our intuition. In life, have you ever felt like you were going in the wrong direction but could not explain why you felt that way? This is your spirit guide trying to show you that alternative routes exist, which must be better, otherwise you would not have had that feeling. When you feel like this, pause, take a deep breath, and then take another look at the path you are choosing. Remember, your spirit guides are not allowed to interfere with your choices, although they can show you options in the hope you will choose well for yourself.

My guide who has been with me from birth is quiet. In his last incarnation, he was a strong Native American Brave, named "Running Waters". He made his presence felt after I had been to a spiritual awareness class. He shared his name and informed me that he was my guardian and had been watching over me from birth. He is my friend in the spirit world. I always sense him standing straight and tall over my right shoulder with a confident smile on his face. I would feel his strong, quiet, protective presence when I needed guidance, gently showing me the way. Shortly afterwards, a few more guides came forth, including a quiet nun, named Mary. Her energy is one of nurturing, compassion, and love. She is quite happy to work behind the scenes, never drawing much attention to herself. She is here to continue her life's work from beyond the veil, aiding and helping the innocents of the world, and does not need to make herself known to do so. Another of my guides is a gentleman whose last incarnation was from the time of the Ming Dynasty, and whose name is Lien. I called him "Lin" for the longest time until he spelled his name out. He appeared in my life as a mentor, sharing his knowledge of herbs, energy, and everything of the earth, which manifested more concretely when I earned certification as a master herbalist and aromatherapist. Lien is loving, quiet and steadfast. I was urged to look up the meaning of his name, which is "lotus flower." I was then told to close my eyes to receive a gift. As the hazy white light cleared, Lien's presence came into sight, bowed, and offered the wonderful affirmation that he was proud of the soul I had become. He outstretched his arms, instantly materializing in the palms of his hand was a beautiful white lotus flower with iridescent droplets of love filled light. The droplets of light washed over my entire being, filling me with feelings of deep gratitude, which coursed through my veins as a tear ran down my cheek. The sacred white lotus flower symbolizes enlightenment, purity, and rebirth. The lotus flower's roots are based in the mud, every night it submerges into the murky water. The next day it pushes through the mud and rises in all its splendor without a hint of struggle or dirt to dull its magnificent blossom, representing our ability to emerge from a place of suffering into the light by improving ourselves with each reemergence.

A few years after meeting these guides, a young Tibetan monk presented himself. It was my dear friend from my prior life as a monk. The spiritual love emanating from his eyes held the whole universe within. He brought to memory that we had a plan and agreed to work together in service to humanity. He was here to assist me in embodying the Rainbow Light Frequencies, alongside Running Waters. Rainbow Light Frequencies occur when you have attained a place of peace, deep understanding, and non-judgment; when deep wounds have been healed and all of your actions come from a place of good intent, your heart is filled with compassion and maintains a constant flow of unconditional love. He was so happy I had not ignored my calling and reassured me that I had fulfilled my mission to date. I was so happy to see my brother, although I do not know his name. When I asked, with a smile he said, "I am you, you are me".

Another spirit guide connected with me that I can only describe as a wisdom keeper. In meditation, he presented himself with eyes full of love and deep knowledge as vast as the ocean itself. Dressed in a cream-colored coarse woven fabric, his sleeves were long and the hemline finished at his ankles, where his feet adorned in open-toed sandals protruded out. In his right hand he held a clear quartz crystal point. It shone so brightly that I sensed it held sacred knowledge of ancient times. He beckoned me to go on a journey to Egypt. We instantly arrived in a small community with an Egyptian Ankh on a hill in the distance. He stated that they originated from Atlantis. He guided me to the entrance of a small clay hut. I stepped in and noticed a table and two stools adjacent to one another in the middle of the cramped space. He gestured for me to sit and then he sat down opposite me. He placed a huge scroll on the table. He unraveled the scroll and I saw there were thousands of names written, but only mine was made clear to see. He said I was one of many souls incarnating at this time to assist in raising the vibration of the third dimensional frequency called the earth plane. He would share his wisdom when it was time for me to receive the information. I felt honored and privileged to be in the presence of such an old wise soul.

Afterwards my mental mind could not rationalize the presence of the Egyptian Ankh in this experience. Did a time exist in human history where an amalgamation between the cultures of ancient Egypt and Atlantis took place? I found out later it was said that some Atlantians had escaped the destruction of their home and settled in Egypt. The world-renowned "Sleeping Prophet", Edgar Cayce, who is considered to be a twentieth-century Nostradamus, revealed in his time that during the final days of Atlantis a mass exodus took place. He explained that the escaping Atlanteans wanted to preserve their history in archives. When they found refuge in Egypt, they also found a place to store their knowledge.

While most of my guides introduced themselves in a more upfront and intrapersonal way, some connected with me through inspiration. In the early 2000's, I was caught off guard with a strong new urge to paint. It was so strong I went out to the shops and bought an easel and various acrylic paints. I sat down in the midst of packages and my mental mind kept thinking *what the heck am I supposed to do with it all!* Vic arrived home from work and, with a puzzled expression on his face asked what on earth I had bought. I told him about my strong urge to paint a picture. Trying to keep a straight face he exclaimed, "you can't even draw a stickman, how are you going to paint a picture?" We both started laughing and I replied, "I don't know but I will."

The next day the urge was so overwhelming I popped into my home office and painted "Wings". This was the first of many. I have three artist spirit guides that inspire me to paint and who channel their magnificent light into the world. I only paint when I am urged to, otherwise it does look like a stickman. The three different styles I channel are spacey, geometric, and angelic.

Professor Bob

ONE GUIDE IN PARTICULAR CAME IN LOUD AND CLEAR. HE GAVE his full name, Robert Jones, but he preferred to be known as Bob. I used to call him "my professor" and he used to jokingly say I was the worst student he had ever had due to my lack of medical knowledge. He was funny and not at all patronizing and our connection was filled with humor. My mediumistic abilities were incredibly strong at this time so the conversations I had with him were crystal clear. I had already looked into his soul and saw the most beautiful benevolent being. This left me in no doubt of his good intentions. One of my mentors had always told me to ask questions and not have blind trust in the unseen. They explained the shadow side can masquerade as light so we have to be discerning. She told me to look into the eyes of the souls introducing themselves and I made it a priority to see each soul's light and to know their intent. I only wanted guides of the highest caliber of light and we have a choice whether we want to work with a guide or not. I asked Bob if he could give more proof of who he was. He said, "go to the local hospital and look me up. I was a professor there before I passed on."

My reply was, "I can't go there looking for a dead professor. They will think I am crazy."

He said, "don't worry, then. I will bring proof to you." I was not expecting much in the form of proof and for the next few weeks I carried on with my life, connecting with my other guides, and looking after my family. I had just returned home from dropping off Oliver at school when the phone rang. A friend of my husband wanted to know if I would offer a reading to someone close to him. I agreed and proceeded to arrange a date and time. The day had come for our meeting and all I could sense from Bob was laughter. I could not understand what he could have found to be so funny and began to suspect there was more to this gathering than I could ever begin to imagine. This became apparent during the session.

Dave and Diane rang the doorbell, entered into our abode, and after a few formalities Diane and I proceeded to the front room where I would be giving her a reading. We hit it off and had a lovely time. I enjoyed connecting with her. Afterwards, Vic and her husband Dave joined us for a cup of tea and a chat. Dave started to enquire how my spiritual path had begun. I went on to explain some of my history and then proceeded to talk about a newer guide, my professor. He was interested in hearing about him and continued to press for more information. I thought it was a little odd as I continued to share the professor's full name, his likes and dislikes, and personal hobbies, even down to the stamp collection my professor had previously told me about. I had not noticed the look on Dave's face until he held his hand up and stopped me from talking. He was as white as a sheet, he started to explain that Professor Bob had been his father's best friend. Not only that, he had Professor Bob's stamp collection in his possession, which he had inherited on his father's passing a few years earlier. We all looked at each other in astonishment. He also informed me that Bob had only died seven years ago and he was the head pathologist at the local hospital; and he actually was a professor; and that he insisted everyone call him Bob. Due to my lack of knowledge of the physical body, my blessed professor had come back swiftly to help his worst student become a spiritual healer, serving with love, light and goodness from my heart. His soul, so loving and kind, chose to come back quickly to the dense energies of this earthly plane to pick up where he left off, bringing the light of Unconditional Love and healing to serve all.

Professor Bob, like the guides I mentioned before, are just a few of the sea of benevolent beings of light I have had the privilege to work with. I always consider myself blessed to be a part of this wondrous team. In addition, I would like to honor the many souls who assist in the healing of all in physical suffering, overseen by a beautiful light, named Hans. In his last incarnation he was a physician, meticulous in his area of expertise and always adorned in his favorite burgundy red bowtie. He supervises and organizes the many spirits who assist in helping physical bodies heal like the chief surgeon of a hospital. Their work is nothing short of miraculous. I have witnessed many miracles over the years and I am always in awe and humbled to be a part of such happenings. My guides always remind me I am the physical anchor. We are one.

The Monk and The Warrior

Oliver and Lewis, my biological sons, have strong empathic and intuitive skills as healers in their own rights. Even while they appear to be polar opposites in personality and interests, they are more alike than they realize. Oliver only ever liked to keep a few friends and actually prefers his own company. We joke that he would be perfectly happy to live on top of a mountain all by himself, surrounded by books, if it was not for his devotion to family. Lewis, on the other hand, was quite popular and social. He could have a gang of friends wherever he went and greatly enjoys fraternity.

Oliver is the kindest, sweetest soul you would ever wish to meet. He never has a bad word to say about anyone. He was born blond-haired and bluey-green-eyed, four days before my twenty-sixth birthday. I could not believe the incredible love I felt holding him in my arms for the first time. I knew and felt he had brought a gift of love, peace, and happiness with him from our Angelic Friends to help us through life's challenges. He was so sweet we called him our little Angel. He was always content, as long as he was cuddled, and I was only too happy to oblige. From the moment he was born, everyone loved him, especially his paternal grandpa, Ernie. They had a special bond from the start. Ernie would tell me that Oliver was so well behaved, he could take him anywhere. From a young age, Oliver used to call Ernie on weekends to talk about sports as Oliver's favorite football team was Manchester United, and Ernie's was Manchester City, hometown rivals to one another.

Oliver's intuitive side started to develop early on. At about four years old, he could sense when friends and family were going to stop by unannounced and would alert me. When he turned five, I thought it was a good idea to talk about stranger-danger. We had a lengthy conversation and Oliver seemed to understand what I was trying to convey. That night I tucked him up in bed, gave him a big hug and kiss and left the room. The next morning, I went to wake him, and to my surprise he was sitting up in bed very alert and looking a little confused. I asked him if he was alright. He said, "Mum, a stranger came to my room last night."

"Oh really?" I replied, "what did he look like?"

"He was all different colors, red, green, blue,"

I asked, "like paint?"

He said, "yes," and with a little smile on his face he went on to say that the stranger's name was George and he was there to look after him. I continued to listen intently, my mind scrabbling to make sense of Oliver's experience, wondering if it was just a dream, when, all of a sudden, he blurted out, "Mum, George also had your friend Bob with him." He then giggled and said, "they are not strangers, are they, Mum? They are our friends."

Astounded, I replied," They are certainly our trusted friends." Oliver had no idea about my spirit guide, Professor Bob. It was a lovely confirmation to know my guide was part of Oliver's introduction to his guide, George. I think this was done to reassure me, and in addition to give proof Oliver was not dreaming.

I sensed George's last incarnation was a strong loving medicine man, indigenous to Australia. I had presumed that George showed himself to Oliver with full body art in many different colors. Personal ornamentation is an ancient tradition and carries a deep spiritual significance for the indigenous people of Australia.

Many years later, I gained a little more clarity on this. Oliver was eleven years old when he rushed into our room in the middle of the night with a frightened look on his face.

"What on earth's the matter?" Vic asked.

"I've just seen a man in army fatigues and a black balaclava covering his head. He walked up the stairs and entered my room," Oliver said.

I reassured Oliver that the lost soul had come because he needed help. The lost soul sensed that Oliver would be able to help him. I soothed Oliver and asked the Angels to help me guide the lost soul to the light.

The next morning, while having breakfast, I asked Oliver if he remembered when George, his spirit guide, first introduced himself. "Of course," he replied, and began describing George like the shape of a physical person with many different colors swirling together, similar to looking through a kaleidoscope.

"Oh, my goodness," I said, "you were actually seeing just his energy. I thought you'd seen him in physical form and his body was painted with body art."

Oliver has always been an empath carrying a beautiful healing light. It was no surprise to me when he decided to become a vegetarian at a young age, or when he became a holistic health practitioner. Oliver specialized in a technique that helps to optimize a person's lymphatic system, called Mizokami Advanced Circulatory Sports Massage (MACSL). He serves those seeking to have their symptoms and pains alleviated from diseases such as rheumatoid arthritis, lupus, Hashimoto's, and various forms and stages of cancer. On more than one occasion, he has been guided to help others find some physical comfort at the end stage of their lives.

We could not be at Ernie's side when he passed over from stage four pancreatic cancer, which devastated us all. A couple of days later, on arriving home after a busy morning of grocery shopping, we parked the car and opened the boot to unload our goods, when we heard loud music coming from across the road. A song we knew all too well was echoing throughout our end of the street as we could clearly make out the lyrics: "*blue moon, you saw me standing alone, without a dream in my heart, without a love of my own. Blue moon, you knew just what I was there for, you heard me saying a prayer for someone I really could care for....*". We looked at one another and smiled knowingly. While our neighbors often blasted music on weekends, the songs had always been in Spanish, usually from the genres of Banda, Mariachi, and Norteño, as Victoria always pointed out the distinctions to us when she reminisced about her own childhood.

The song, "Blue Moon", originally written in 1934, is the Manchester City Football Club's anthem, and one of Ernie's favorite songs. The next day, Vic shared this wonderful message with his mum. She informed him that she had already chosen "Blue Moon" to play at Ernie's funeral.

A few months later, Oliver's oldest son, Ollie, who was only two and a half years old at the time, started staring at the window by the front door, giggling and chatting to an invisible visitor. Some days after that incident, while we were gathering around the dining table, Ollie shouted out, "Ernest!" from his highchair. We were gobsmacked. Ollie was pleased with himself that he got the name out clearly. He was still learning how to speak. We had never referred to Ernie as anything other than Grandad, Dad, or just Ernie. Ernie had come through to Ollie to let us know that he was checking in on us and to comfort us, knowing that we had taken the news of his death hard. It was also a message to Oliver that their bond was not broken when he left this earthly realm.

I always wanted more than one biological child. Ideally, I would have loved a house full of children. Alas, money had been tight and life was incredibly busy. Vic had started his own business and in no time at all he and I were chugging along in our thirties. My biological clock was ticking away. We decided to try for another child after much deliberation. I became pregnant right away, but picked up the feeling this baby was not meant to stay. I miscarried at around ten weeks. I can remember sitting in a hospital bed with complications and feeling the exact moment that the soul of my unborn child left. It was a sad and strange feeling, almost like the soul had moved through me. After the loss, my hormones went haywire and I began to doubt if I would ever conceive again.

My Angelic Friends stepped in to reassure me that I would, indeed, have another. It was in October of 1996 when they said, "Tracey you will have your baby in the fall." I relaxed and got on with my life, surrendering any expectations. In March, 1997, I sat in the bathroom with a pregnancy test, and waited for what felt like an eternity for the lines to appear. It is amazing what two little blues can mean to a person.

I yelled to Vic, "I'm pregnant!" I was beside myself with excitement and deep gratitude. What a beautiful birthday blessing I had received. Even though I had a scare during the first trimester, I knew in my heart our baby was here to stay. The weeks passed and the bond I felt with the life forming inside of me was an incredibly deep love. I knew he was a special little rainbow baby.

While heavily pregnant, I received a message from my dear intuitive friend, Barbara. She said that our son would be a spiritual warrior. We did not know the sex of our baby at the time. She explained that he had been a soldier in his previous life fighting for peace. She also told me he would be born with a specific birthmark on the back of his head, a remnant of an injury from his past life. That November, our blond-haired little boy with bright green eyes was born. Lewis came into the world with a blast. I was in labour for less than an hour. As I held my beautiful little boy, my heart overwhelmed with love for this tiny little being, I noticed a small, crimson red, circular birthmark in the nape of his neck. Barbara's prediction came flooding back. As I cradled Lewis in my arms, I felt his soul; his strong, bright, loving, fearless spirit; and his warrior energy.

Lewis's intuitive and healing skills came to light on his first birthday. We had thrown a little party at home. My sister Sarah had come to pick up her son. We were chatting merrily about the day's events while the boys played with all the new toys, when all of a sudden Lewis, six months younger than his cousin, placed his hands over the top of his cousin's head. Sarah's son had crouched down and for a few minutes, time stood still. Neither one moved, except for Lewis's tiny hands when they involuntarily started to shake. Sarah looked at me with her mouth wide open. She exclaimed, "what on earth is he doing?"

By this point I could psychically see the stream of divine light flowing from his little hands. I replied, "he is giving him energy healing." I was also shocked. Sarah's son had been born ten weeks premature. His little lungs had collapsed and he had suffered a small bleed and had swelling on his brain. The doctors were not sure if he would be left with any permanent brain damage. He grew up without any disabilities. I sensed that these two souls, born just six months apart, had an agreement before incarnating that if his cousin was struggling with his physical body, then Lewis would step in to help him energetically.

When Lewis was three years old, we received another message from a Romani card reader at a local outdoor market. He laid three playing cards out before me, turned one over, looked me in the eye, and said: "your son will wear a military uniform." Over the years, we observed Lewis and wondered if he would step onto the path his soul had once experienced? Could we make a difference by encouraging him to take a different route? I was not sure but certainly tried my best. When he turned eight, we had a family outing to a visiting fair. As we walked by the attractions, Lewis's attention was drawn to a little rifle range. He wanted to see if he could hit the bullseye. We let him try, not expecting him to hit anything. He picked up the rifle and on his first attempt he hit that bullseye. There was no doubt in our minds that he had done it before. We pushed it all to the back of our minds and got on with life. Lewis used to tell me he knew things before they happened. This went on for quite a number of years. His happy go lucky persona was quite a hit with his peers and he had started to goof around a lot, especially in class. He always made everyone laugh.

Upon entering his teenage years, he was adamant about joining the armed forces. I explained to him that feelings of unfinished business from his prior life could be a driving force in him wanting to make this decision, and he did not have to follow that path again. A few more years of going back and forth, we thought he might have decided against it.

In January of 2018, as I was packing in preparation for our move. Lewis caught me with my guard down. "Mum, I have joined the Army," he said. I cried for a week. Like any other mother, I did not want my baby boy put into any dangerous situations, and I knew that it would be some time before we could have him home again. Lewis left for boot camp eight months later. Waving goodbye to our youngest son was heart wrenching. We wished him well on his journey with feelings of deep love, sadness, and a little fear in our hearts. But, most of all, we are proud of him for following his heart.

When it came time for him to start his service, we left Lewis all alone in a hotel room in San Diego. He would be flying to boot camp in Georgia in the early hours of the morning. While waiting to leave, he received a call via Facebook messenger. Vic's brother had not been able to get a hold of Vic and he saw that Lewis was available online. He delivered the devastating news that his grandma Ettie had just died. He had no idea that Lewis was not at home and he wanted to reach Vic before word got out on social media. We felt so bad for Lewis, he had to be the one to break the news to us just as he was about to spend four months with extremely limited contact with his family, knowing his grandma had just died.

I often called on the Archangel Michael, patron saint of those who work in perilous conditions, such as soldiers and police officers, to intercede for and protect Lewis. I received confirmation from my dear friend, Sherae, that Archangel Michael had heard my prayers when she sent me a message saying, Archangel Michael considers Lewis, "one of his own." As I always do when receiving profound messages, I pondered it, and was in gratitude for the divine help.

Lewis clearly had unfinished business and unresolved issues from his previous incarnation. He needed to experience something that was started in his prior lifetime to find peace in this one. His grandma left this world and took on a special job as a guiding light, illuminating his path, with his guardian Angels, who have yet to reveal themselves, but I sense they will very soon. After dutifully serving his time in the U.S. Army, he is currently phasing out of service to start a new chapter of his life with his wife, Zoe, and precious newborn son, Beau, whom we were blessed and thrilled to welcome into our family on September 29, 2021.

Beau's auspicious birthday was another message of divine protection from the angels. We had expected his arrival on an earlier date, but he held out for just the right moment. September 29th is known as the beginning of celebrations for the Feast of Saints Michael, Gabriel, and Raphael, and sometimes Uriel. Traditionally, St. Michael's Day has been celebrated since the fifth century. This day was used to draw strength from the Archangels and pray for protection over families through the winter months to come. I am in no doubt that the Archangel Michael sent his love with Beau and placed a sparkle of divine light in Lewis's heart.

The Butterfly

I WAS TWENTY-THREE YEARS OLD WHEN I MET MY SOULMATE, VIC. The spark of recognition between us was so strong we both intuitively knew we were destined to be together and, after a whirlwind romance, we married in 1988. The day I met Clair and Alex, who were seven and three years old at the time—I was struck by their stunning blue eyes. They were beautiful children. Clair was destined to stand out wherever she was with her gorgeous mop of blond curls. I was wearing a butterfly brooch on that day and Clair took a liking to the sparkly piece filled with colorful crystals. I gave it to her knowing our first meeting had created a bond never to be broken.

I became a second mum to Clair and Alex. Clair was a little chatterbox. Vic used to say she needed a blowhole at the top of her head like a dolphin so she could breathe between words. She was affectionate, inquisitive, feisty, and caring; and was always willing to help in any way she could. I found it sweet and funny when she made it a habit of always plopping down between Vic and I when we would sit together. Alex, on the other hand, was quieter than Clair, except for when the opportunity to sing presented itself. He was quite steadfast, self-assured, athletic, strong, and loving. I tried my best to be a good step-mum, knowing very well what it felt like to be a stepchild. Less than two years later, we were blessed with the birth of Oliver, and Lewis was born seven years after. Each child came with an abundance of love to offer the world and we had our hands full.

In 2006, we were living on Thorpe Lane, in Austerlands, in a big red brick house that sat high up on a hill from which one could see all of the fireworks on Bonfire Night across England all the way to Wales. Vic was running the structural engineering business he had started many years prior, where he employed Clair as his bookkeeper while she was studying to become an accountant. She was intelligent and keen. Her strong personality earned her a reputation among the men on the steel shop floor. They used to refer to her as a "rottweiler" and would often say that nothing could get past her, especially while doing payroll. When the workers would try to say they had done more hours than they had; she could recount to them what jobs were going on and how many hours were actually worked to get each job done, firmly putting anyone in their place. She was Vic's right-hand-girl and was proud of that fact.

Only months prior, towards the end of 2005, Clair had developed a limp and began to lose her balance from time to time. The limp gradually progressed until she was falling regularly. She had also been losing her grip on objects throughout the day. Out of concern, we asked her to see a doctor. She told us that she had seen a doctor and she was told that her problem was a trapped nerve. Pushing worry to the side, she spoke often about planning a wedding, wanting to marry her fiancé, Matt, whom she had been exclusively seeing since she was seventeen years old. Together they shared a daughter, Kaya, who was about to turn one year old. With Oliver's sixteenth birthday quickly approaching; Clair was only one exam from becoming an accountant; talked about planning a wedding for her and Matt; and the first birthday of our first granddaughter, we had much to be grateful for and to look forward to in 2006.

However, the truth of the matter was that Clair had not seen a doctor, and her symptoms worsened. She could no longer avoid seeking medical help. Clair was only twenty-five years old when she was diagnosed with a grade four glioblastoma. The news devastated us all. She was the second member of the O'Mara family to be diagnosed with a brain tumor and the third young member of the family to develop cancer. Vic's nephew, Jonathan, had passed at the tender age of six, twenty-five years before, and Catherine, Vic's cousin battled bone cancer for many years until she passed at the age of seventeen.

We went into overdrive that March to support Clair, Matt, and Kaya in any way we could. Being the brave and courageous young woman she was, and without a thought for herself, Clair decided to raise money for a children's cancer foundation by shaving off her glorious curly blond locks. Her philosophy was, if these brave little children can fight cancer and beat it, so could she.

While undergoing daily doctor visits and cycles of chemo and radiotherapy, Clair was still looking at dresses and possible destinations for a wedding when she recovered. We shared many conversations during car rides to and from the doctor's office about how she would like her special day. One Saturday in July, I received a phone call from Matt asking me to pick up Kaya. He had found Clair convulsing on the bathroom floor. As I pulled up to their house, Clair was being lifted into the ambulance. Vic and Oliver, who were both working nearby, arrived minutes before the ambulance, while Clair was still in the midst of her convulsions. Vic and Matt followed Clair to the hospital, where Clair was admitted to the intensive care unit. I took Oliver, Lewis, and Kaya to Vic's parents' house. From there I drove to Clair's mum's house, bringing her with me to meet Vic and Matt at the hospital, where we waited together for news from the doctor. Clair had suffered a grand mal seizure. She had fallen into a coma and the doctors told us she would not come out of it. The doctors must not have been informed of Clair's might. Through the strength of her will, Clair pulled out of her coma. The seizure had robbed Clair of her ability to walk and caused numbness in her right arm. She was no longer able to care for herself.

The chaos of that event changed us all. After a few weeks in the hospital, it was decided that Clair would move in with us until she was well enough to leave so that she and Matt could be better supported. We converted our downstairs office into a bedroom and kitted it out with the specialized equipment loaned to us from the medical facility. Her mum had recently moved into a smaller space and, despite all of her efforts, did not have capacity for all of the medical equipment, no matter how she would have tried to make it fit. Not being able to house Clair was agonizing for her. I reassured Clair's mum that she would be welcome in our home and we could all nurse and care for Clair together.

Clair's mum, Matt, Vic, and I formed a team of care for Clair and for one another. We each had our own roles to fill. Vic and Matt worked full time in order to provide for their respective families. Clair's mum had taken a long-term absence from her job to care for her daughter. Matt would drop Clair's mum off at our house in the morning, after taking Kaya to nursery school, in time for me to take Lewis to school and return home again. Together, Clair's mum and I provided direct round-the-clock care for Clair: washing the bedding daily, administering medicine, cooking and cleaning, and meeting any of her needs and the needs of the other members of our family. In the evening, Matt would pick up Kaya and bring home the dinners that Ettie, Vic's mum, had made for us all. Then, Matt would take Clair's mum home and I would offer readings for people in the evening, whenever I could, and look after our other children. This cycle would repeat daily. Additionally, I kept a baby monitor on throughout the night so that I could respond quickly to Clair's needs. As well as giving her regular energy healing treatments, I used to massage her feet and legs with lavender oil to help increase circulation. The massage brought her some relief and it made me happy knowing I could help ease any of her pain, even if it was in a small way.

After a couple of months of our new routine, I found myself momentarily dozing off during a reading and after that decided that I should stop going out to work in the evenings. It was around this time the Marie Curie nurses offered us respite by sending a nurse nightly so that I could sleep soundly, knowing that Clair was in good hands. They were a godsend.

We knew that we had to be present for Clair in a way that would not emotionally distress her. The seizure had left her with short-term memory loss, which could be both a blessing and a curse. On one hand, she did not always realize how sick she was or how long she had been immobilized and therefore was unable to dwell on her circumstances; on the other hand, she was unable to remember things from only a minute before in some instances. When her daughter, Kaya, cried, Clair would try to get out of bed having forgotten that she could not walk. In those moments the realization of her situation would dawn on her. Seconds would pass and she would forget it all again. Clair did, however, retain her fantastic sense of humor. She would request to watch the same comedy several times a day, not realizing she had already watched it. We often saw her rolling with laughter at the same scenes over and over again which would send the rest of us into fits of giggles. Clair had difficulty getting her words out, but for some reason or another, she had acquired a colorful mastery of the word, "fuck". We made a swear box for her and placed it on the windowsill. As that box filled up, we promised we would take her out as soon as she felt better. I am grateful to have shared these moments of laughter in a time that was so dark for us.

My sister, Sarah, called me one day in the midst of all of this. Her fiancé had suddenly died, he was forty-four years old. It was at this point I stopped and asked the Universe: *What is going on?*

By the end of the summer, Vic came to me and, with a deep sadness in his voice, he said, "she's going to pass on her birthday, Tracey. I just know." Clair's birthday was New Year's Eve. In November, Clair's medical specialist requested a meeting with us. The doctor informed us that Clair would not be on the earth for much longer. Immediately following the news, Vic and I asked Clair's mum to move in with us, so that mother and daughter could spend as much time together as possible.

Despite all of our intentions, and all of the compromises being made to mutually support one another within the family, some things were bound to give now and again. Lewis was still in primary school and with the full-time care that Clair needed, we did not have the time or resources to be consistent with his homework. In regard to Lewis, our focus had been on maintaining his mental and emotional health, given the circumstances. After a discussion with his teacher to fill her in on the dire situation our family was facing, we informed her that we would try our best to meet all of Lewis's academic responsibilities, and conveyed that if he missed a homework assignment, it was our fault, not his. I specifically asked her not to punish him for this and that we would try to make up any missing assignments. Not two days after this meeting, I picked up Lewis from school. He was upset. He had been given detention for not turning in his homework and his lunch time had been revoked for him to serve this punishment. I confronted his teacher and headteacher who patronized and minimized what we were going through. His headteacher responded to my concerns with: "oh, I understand there is pressure at home because I had some health issues as well." She then explained how she had survived breast cancer. I let her know that I had compassion and empathy for what she had gone through, but she did not fully understand the severity of our situation. She implied that a good mother would consistently spend time with her children on their homework. I left the school grounds feeling terribly small, much as Lewis did when I picked him up. When information regarding this exchange at school got back to the Macmillan nurses, the specialist cancer and palliative care team looking after Clair who were intimately aware of Clair's case, they were horrified and immediately contacted the education board to request one of their school nurses report to Lewis's school to keep an eye on him for his emotional wellness.

While I had deep gratitude for the Macmillan nurses and their support and advocacy, the conflict with Lewis's teacher and headteacher wounded me. I was angry, and found it unbelievable that two intelligent people could lack compassion for an eight-year-old child who was witnessing his sister's last weeks on earth, and who had been witnessing her decline over the last several months. I asked the Angels and my spirit guides to help me overcome the unnecessary additional emotional turmoil. I felt the energy of a warm blanket being placed on my shoulders to reassure me of their presence. My guides asked me to have forgiveness for those incapable of understanding the ways they can burden others with unkind words and attitudes.

The weeks went by and Christmas Day was soon upon, bringing a wonderful love-filled celebration. Family from all sides visited us, coming and going throughout the day. Clair seemed brighter than normal and extremely happy to see so many of her loved ones. She was fully enjoying the Christmas spirit.

The next day, Clair slipped into a coma. Our hearts sank. We knew she could not stay much longer and that her battle was too big to overcome. We all sensed that she was waiting for Vic's brother, Craig, and his wife, Yvette, to visit from London. She had not seen them at Christmas as they always came to visit on New Year's Eve instead.

It was New Year's Eve, 2006, and Clair's twenty-sixth birthday. I was dabbing Clair's lips with a little yellow sponge filled with water to stop them from drying out, when I heard Craig and Yvette's voices. Vic guided them to the entrance of the room. I could see the shock on their faces. The full severity of her circumstance hit them hard. Craig stepped into the room and went to Clair's bedside to speak to her. He gave her a hug and stepped out of the room with tears in his eyes. They left twenty minutes later to meet up with Vic's mum and dad. Oliver and Lewis had been staying with them for a few days and we were hoping this would distract them. They had all gone to watch our nephew, Gavin, sing at a local conservative club.

After Craig left at 11:00 PM, I whispered in Clair's ear, "Clair, listen to everyone chatting merrily, they will be fine. Don't stay for us, you have seen everyone. Now you need to go with the Angels to the light. We love you."

Soon after, Vic, Clair's mum, and her mum's sister joined me. Matt and Alex continued chatting in the living room and said they would be joining us shortly. I moved to the chair at the foot of the bed, facing Clair, and Vic followed. Clair's mum and aunt sat on either side of her. In the midst of conversation, Vic and I looked at each other, we had both noticed Clair's breathing had changed. I looked at my watch. It was nearly 11:20 PM. A few moments later we watched her take her last peaceful breath.

While Clair's mum and Matt spent individual time with Clair, we set off to break the heartbreaking news to Oliver and Lewis. Vic had already called his brother in order to prepare his Mum and Dad. News travels fast in a group of small villages and we did not want them to overhear any gossip. On entering the busy club, bathed in streamers and party poppers, Gavin's voice lifted over the noisy crowd with the lyrics, "goodbye my friend, it's hard to die, when all the birds are singing in the sky." He was singing Terry Jack's "Seasons in The Sun". When he saw us, his singing stopped and tears filled his eyes. He had lost his brother, Jonathan, when he was only eight years old, and now his cousin. The looks on our faces must have brought a multitude of painful memories back. Catherine's mum, Yvonne, recognizing the expressions on our faces, walked over to us, gave us a huge hug, strong and tight, and a glass of wine. I knocked it back in one go and walked over to where the rest of the family sat.

Sharing the news with Oliver and Lewis in a busy place was not what we had planned, but being surrounded by their cousins and loving older family members gave them incredible strength to deal with the devastating news. They decided to stay with their grandparents and the rest of the family and we made our way back home.

The house was filled with a sadness no words could begin to describe. Vic and I spent more time with Clair. I had called the medical team before leaving to share the news of Clair's death. The district nurses had arranged to come and help me prepare Clair's body. I also had an agreement with her doctor that if she passed in the night, I would send him a text message and we would wait for him to come in the morning. We were warned that if we called the out-of-hours doctor, he would not be familiar with the case, and by law he would have to bring the police to search Clair's body. I was not going to let that happen to her.

Vic, Clair's mum, Alex and Matthew had all crashed out from the shock by the time the nurse arrived. I had made a silent promise to Clair that I would not leave her until the doctor came. The nurse was so supportive, making sure the family and I were stable before we started tending to Clair. She gently and quickly removed all of the medical paraphernalia. We then washed and dressed Clair. I put her warm fluffy socks on. I could never stand the thought of her feet being cold.

The nurse made me a hot cup of tea sweetened with honey, hugged me, and left. I sat alone in deep thought when suddenly the vase situated on a side table was knocked and the flowers began to shake. I knew then I was not alone, my Angelic Friends were letting me know I was being supported and Clair was with them. Clair's aunt returned from sharing the news with their side of the family and joined me. We sat together through the night waiting. She was concerned that I had not called the out-of-hours doctor. I reassured her that I knew what I was doing. I had absolute trust in Clair's doctor, even though I had not received a reply.

On New Year's Day, Clair's doctor came to pronounce her dead. The undertaker came in to remove her body from the home. After all of the care that Clair's mum, Vic, Matt, and I had lovingly provided; after all of the thought and consideration we had put into making sure that the body that had served the soul of our precious girl was properly honored and treated, it was a knife in the heart for me to watch it zipped up in this horrible burgundy body bag. Clair's mum, aunt, and I stood with our arms around one another watching as they carried her out just like they would with any other body.

Two days later, I was looking at the clear crystal dolphin Clair had gifted me earlier that same year, when I thought I heard a knock at the front door. No one was there. I peered around and watched as a beautiful butterfly promptly flew into our home. I had never seen a butterfly in the wet and freezing temperatures of the UK winter before. It was a message from Clair.

Vic, Matt and I sat on the sofa together not many days after. Oliver, Lewis, and Kaya were all in bed fast asleep. Kaya had a little cooker that made a buzzing noise when the small toy pan was placed on it. Our conversation about Clair's celebration of life was suddenly interrupted when the toy cooker began to buzz. We all jumped at the unexpected sound. Clair made her presence known by sitting down in between Vic and I. He looked at me and said "Clair's here, I can feel her!"

I then heard Clair say that she loved the special ring Matthew had ordered for her. She said it had an inscription inside and three diamonds. "Does this make any sense to you?" I asked Matt.

He replied sheepishly, "yes. I've got the ring coming tomorrow." He wanted to put it on Clair's finger at the chapel of rest. He had not told a single person. We were all astonished, not just to have Clair's spirit visit us so soon, but to pass a message through me was mind blowing. I did not think she could have told me anything that I did not already know, teaching me never to presume anything. The power of love had brought her back swiftly to help her family in our time of grief giving us the reassurance of her soul's continuing existence in another realm. Clair absolutely adored her little girl. I have no doubt she came back to check on her and bless her with the light of love emanating from her pure heart.

Less than three weeks after Clair's funeral, I was on my normal route to pick Lewis up from school. Two of my friends were at the school also picking up their children. Upon seeing me, their brows furrowed with concern and worry etched across their faces. They stopped me in passing to warn me about what had been done during the school day and what I would find in Lewis's backpack. To meet curriculum requirements in language arts, the teacher had decided that the children would learn what an epitaph was by creating one for themselves. I pulled a paper headstone out of Lewis's backpack with his name written on the front. Not long after standing next to his sister's headstone, Lewis was asked to bring one home of his own. Had I not received the warning from my friends, I know that the shock of this would have devastated me. I felt the warm blanket of the Angels comforting me once again and their words ringing through my ears to forgive his teacher.

A couple of months went by when I received another message that Clair was checking in on us. I was visiting with my dear friend, Joyce, when she exclaimed, "Clair's here bringing her love to you and showing me a dolphin and these big fluffy socks and saying, 'thank you'. Do you understand the message, Tracey?"

With tears rolling down my face I whispered, "yes I do." In addition to the crystal dolphin Clair bought me, I also had a little rose quartz dolphin, which Clair loved. I gave the rose quartz dolphin to her at the chapel of rest. Joyce then said, "she will send you one back via someone else." One of my dear friends gave me a rose quartz dolphin a few years later without knowing of its importance. I have received three more since, and a pink glass dolphin from Oliver's mother-in-law. Clair has been busy.

Within three months of Clair's passing, Alex's first-born, Jonathan, who was only a baby, developed bacterial meningitis. It was a frightening time for the family, especially for Alex, who had just lost his sister, and was now watching his son fight for his life in the hospital. I had faith he would pull through and he did, after all, he had a special Angel watching over him.

Meanwhile, Mum's drinking was escalating and I was on pins wondering what would happen next. Sure enough, Mum got herself arrested. Mum and Peter had been going through a nasty divorce when his father passed away. Mum had never got along with Peter's dad. I had begged mum not to show up at the funeral. She promised she would stay away. I called Mum around 9:00 AM on the day of the funeral to remind her of her promise. Her response was: "I'm going and no one can stop me!" She was already drunk.

I did not attend the funeral. I had not interacted much with Peter or his dad and had been far too consumed with everything else going on. Knowing that Mum would be making an appearance at the funeral, I anxiously waited for the bomb to drop. The phone rang. I answered. It was my sister, Sarah.

"Holy fuck!" Sarah screamed on the other end, "Mum's turned up to church with Bruce!" I cringed, picturing Bruce, Mum's Neapolitan Mastiff, in the church like a bull in a china shop. Sarah continued shouting, "she stood in the door way and said, 'where the fuck is Humpty-Dumpty?'" Mum was referring to Peter. "Then, someone, 'yelled get that dog out of here!' and Mum yelled back, 'why? Isn't it God's house and doesn't he welcome all creatures great and small?" Pandemonium ensued.

Mum was arrested and spent the day at the police station. I eventually tracked her down and the sergeant said she had been driving everyone crazy. Frustrated, the sergeant asked, "can't anyone keep her under control?"

"We've certainly tried," I replied, "have you any ideas?" Sarah and I were mortified, but it must have been so much worse for Peter and my youngest sister, Maria.

Six months after Clair died, my cousin lost a long battle with skin cancer at the age of forty-five. Ten months after Clair died, Alex was involved in a horrific car accident. Alex and two of his friends had been out drinking. They were heading home in the early hours of the morning and the car swerved and crashed into a barrier. Alex was sitting in the middle of the backseat with just a lap belt on. The impact of the crash caused a ruptured spleen and damage to his colon and shoulder. The driver, fearing he would be over the legal limit for alcohol, panicked and ran. The other passenger followed. Neither had seen Alex collapse while trying to exit the car. A lone taxi driver had just dropped off his customer and was heading home when he witnessed the crash. He went to Alex's aid and stayed with him until the ambulance arrived. Thank God that he did! The injuries he sustained were life threatening. Alex was rushed straight to the hospital where emergency surgery was performed to stop the internal bleeding. He spent a few days in intensive care and eventually made a full recovery, but still deals with the pain and scars from that night.

Was it luck or divine intervention? I am as certain as I can be that Clair had a hand in protecting her younger brother that night. The outcome could have been so much worse. The thought that our family could have lost two children and a grandchild in the space of twelve months was mentally and emotionally taxing, to say the least. We are so grateful to the taxi driver that ran to Alex's side for not leaving him alone in the state he was in and staying with him until he was in safe hands.

I am honored and blessed to call myself Clair and Alex's step-mum. I have always tried my best. I have made mistakes, but I have tried to learn and to grow in every way. Through the challenges, I gained a greater understanding of the role of my own stepfathers. I could see all sides of the picture. It is an amazing view when you see through positive eyes.

As painful as it was for me to lose Clair, a stepdaughter I loved and cherished, being one step removed gave me the strength to not only care for Clair, but also to support everyone on an emotional level in the best way that I could. Together as a family we changed our individual priorities enough to get us through. My heart went out every day to Vic and Clair's mum, as the pain of losing a child, no matter the age of that child, is almost unbearable.

One day, Oliver, who was sixteen years old at the time, stopped me and said, "do you know how strong you are, Mum?"

"Really?" I said, "do you think so?"

He replied, "look at what you've been through." That was the first time any person had ever said that to me. It was like a lightbulb was turned on in my mind. His statement opened the door for me to look at myself through new eyes and, in that moment, I saw myself as a courageous person with strength and grit, rather than the super sensitive, overly emotional person I had formerly labeled myself. I was given a new perspective that I was the champion of my story and I could work to overcome anything with a positive disposition.

Vic and I have been blessed to have had such wonderful and encouraging children. For our thirty-first wedding anniversary, we received a message from Alex that contained a poem. He wrote:

> *Biological dad,*
> *Some say step-mum,*
> *Not in my eyes,*
> *Not even some.*
> *You were always there,*
> *In good times or bad,*
> *You took in your heart,*
> *This crazy young lad.*
> *Thirty-one years gone by,*
> *You're still much in love,*
> *It seems to me,*
> *You both fit like a glove.*
> *So from Clair, Al, Oli and Lew,*
> *We'd just like to say that we'll always love you.*

This came straight from his loved-filled heart, and I think Clair had also given him a nudge. She always made a point of sending us an anniversary card.

Off the Wagon

MUM HAD ALWAYS LIKED TO HAVE A DRINK OR TWO. EVERY evening, she would have a tipple. It quickly increased to a 2-litre bottle of cider a night. Mum worked hard and the habitual drinking did not appear to negatively affect her work or social life at first. Growing up, we never knew anything else, so it was our "normal". After retiring, her alcohol consumption had been left unchecked and escalated to epic proportions, which eventually led to the breakdown of her twenty-eight-year marriage to Peter. Alcoholism took a hold of Mum. Her mood swings could range from mild to severe and I never knew how she would respond to interactions with me. On one occasion, I had stopped by to visit her at home. She was slouched on the settee in a terrible state. Her hair was matted and her appearance disheveled. She had been in the same place on the couch and in the same clothes for at least two days. The Righteous Brothers song, "Unchained Melody" played on repeat for at least as long as I was there, and probably for as long as she had been on that settee.

Deeply concerned, I sat down and tried to start a conversation with her. She responded to me with such venom, shouting, name calling, and accusing me of things that were painful to hear coming from anyone, especially my Mum. I started to fall into a place of victimhood and began to feel sorry for myself when my Angelic Friends said, "Tracey, look into her eyes. Can't you see what's happening here?"

I looked in her eyes and saw that she was being manipulated by a darker energy; this was not Mum interacting with me. She was being used to attack me. I wrapped her in divine light, excused myself and left. I returned to her home two hours later to find Mum was back in control and cheery. This time telling me that I was the sweetest daughter on the planet. She had no recollection of our previous meeting earlier that same day. This was a great lesson for me. Once I had understood where her aggression was coming from, I was able to come from a place of non-reaction and removed myself from any more aggressive personal attacks. I gained wisdom through my experience. She helped me understand how easily we can be manipulated by shadow energies.

When Mum consumed copious amounts of alcohol, the essence of her soul left her body for a short period, leaving her body susceptible to low vibrational entities. This can be why those who overindulge sometimes experience blacking out, a drug or alcohol induced state where they are unable to recall certain events and seem to lose control of themselves for a period of time. Aside from the physiological ways alcohol affects the hippocampus, which disrupts memory, and neuroreceptors such as dopamine and serotonin, which regulate mood, there can also be metaphysical consequences to alcohol abuse. When too much alcohol is consumed, the living environment of the physical body becomes too toxic for the soul to thrive in. The soul leaves the body and stays connected by a thin, golden and silver strand. This allows the lower vibrational entities, often abusive and self-serving, to take over. For these spirits, our bodies are vessels to use for mischievous adventures, creating mayhem in their wake.

It is my belief that this is why a person usually forgets or becomes unaware of their actions and behavior when overloaded with alcohol. Relatives and friends have a terrible time dealing with their loved one's alcoholism, not understanding the full complexity of the situation. Alcoholism is a serious, complicated, and understated medical condition with both physical and psychological explanations and ramifications. However, the metaphysical component of overshadowing, when an entity temporarily places itself at the forefront of another soul's physical experience by using their body, can sometimes, but not always, be at play in negative altercations with alcoholics. The entity achieves this agreement through manipulation. Not in full awareness due to the effects alcohol has on the mind and the free feeling the soul has from being slightly liberated from the body, the soul must have, under false pretenses, given permission to the entity to use their body. No entity can ever enter the body of another person without permission from the soul it belongs to, first.

This metaphysical component is not an excuse for the harmful behaviors of those suffering from alcoholism, who need to find the strength to ask for the help necessary to take back control and responsibility over their lives. I find the majority of souls addicted to certain substances to be loving, kind, and extremely gentle. They tend to find life's challenges on earth incredibly hard. Substance abuse gives them the false sense of release. Once hooked, they perpetuate a cycle of addiction, never seeing the escape ladder attached to the wall of the dark pit they have trapped themselves in. The Angels are forever illuminating the ladder for these souls, thus encouraging them to take the first step. Remember: we all have free will, so unless a person chooses to recognize and step on the ladder, there is not much their loved ones can do to help them. The lesson I gleaned from this was if I could deal with Mum being manipulated and overcome it, I could deal with any lower vibrational being.

I love Mum, but I would not allow myself to be attacked or to be drawn into negative feelings or behavior. I found that by loving Mum without condoning or being privy to her negative behavior I was able to move forward from this issue without building resentment or creating a narrative for myself based on self-pity.

After many more episodes, I persuaded Mum to go into rehab. Her sobriety lasted nine weeks. When she relapsed, she stated firmly, "Tracey, I want to kill myself with alcohol and there's nothing you or anyone else can do to stop me."

"Okay," I said, "I'll love you, regardless." I knew I could not help her anymore. I had to surrender any hope of her overcoming her addiction.

Mum had some lovely jewelry and I received a message from spirit that it would be stolen. I asked her if I could safeguard her precious gems and heirlooms. She agreed. My brother did not like this suggestion. He thought it would be best kept in her safe. At this time, Mum had been letting a lot of younger people come into her home to drink alcohol. She believed they were her friends and we, her children, were the enemy. She also had given them her PIN number to her bank card. They had managed to draw and spend £3000 before we found out. My hopes in humanity were dimmed by many awful events. Even the mobile man selling frozen seafood took advantage of her inebriated state, he sold mum £600 worth of fish. Her fridge was fit to burst. I was furious. I called him to complain and told him he should be ashamed of himself. He stuttered over his words saying my mum had insisted she wanted it all. What else could I do? She would not listen to any reason.

My brother Lee decided to move back in with Mum. This was a relief, at least he would keep an eye on her and who she was allowing into the house. I was pressured by both of them against my better judgement to return her jewelry for Lee to lock in Mum's safe. While helping Mum through her divorce, I proceeded with my plans to emigrate. We had sold the house and two days before we left England, Mum was in the ER suffering from hallucinations. The next day, her consultant called to give me an update, which was completely out of character and unexpected. As we chatted, I explained I was leaving the country and that I felt awful abandoning her. He assured me, "go with confidence you cannot help your mum." I found it bizarre, consultants in the UK do not typically call offspring, especially regarding someone in Mum's circumstance. I am confident he was prompted by the Angels to help reassure me of my decision.

Saying goodbye to Mum was so hard. She told me I would never be happy in California. I knew it was another little dig from grey energy. When we parted, she gave me a beautiful Victorian opal necklace, one of her precious heirlooms. She insisted I take it. I am so glad I did. A few weeks later, all of the jewelry left in her safe, about £12,000 worth, were stolen.

Years later, I took the necklace to an opal dealer and he exclaimed, "do you know what you have here?" He went on to explain the opal was from an old mine closed more than one hundred years before. Apparently, it was quite the collector's item.

At some point, Mum decided to sell her house. Within three months of that decision, £80,000 evaporated, stolen by her "friends". Although she had moved into another home she was renting, she spent time living in the park. She told me she "met a better class of people there." During this time, we had no idea where she was. I was thousands of miles away and out of my mind with worry. Vic's best friend, Mick, a police officer of many years, was the kind soul who found Mum drunk and covered in muck in the park. Mick's wife, Kath, immediately called to let us know Mum was safe. Mick also helped bring justice to a man who had stolen money from Mum's purse. Two men had been chatting to her in a local pub. She left her purse on the bar while visiting the restroom, they stole a few thousand pounds out of it and one of them splurged on a vacation to Spain with his ill-gotten gains. Call it coincidence, if you like, I am absolutely sure Mick was guided by the Angels to help find mum and bring her to safety. I am eternally grateful for Mick and Kath's kindness and friendship and the priceless gift of peace of mind given to us when he rescued mum.

Today, Mum and I speak once a week on the phone. Despite having survived breast cancer, a stroke, which has restricted movement on the left side of her body, and a broken collar bone due to osteoporosis, she is happy and settled in a secure nursing home where they call her "Madgic" and she is treated like a queen bee, enjoying a couple of light beers per day. Since Mum's alcohol intake has been restricted and managed by the care home, her innate positivity has been able to shine through, allowing her to find her inner strength and peace. Her new motto is, "que sera, sera". I have only had positive interactions with her since she moved into this facility. In my eyes, the caregivers are all earth Angels.

A number of my relatives have had their battles with substance abuse. Fortunately, my sister's story is one of triumph. Sarah was only in her early thirties when she succumbed to alcohol addiction in a misguided effort to ignore and escape the problems she was enduring in a mentally and physically abusive relationship. Her husband at the time was unkind to both her and her small son from her prior marriage. His cruel tendencies, controlling ways, and drinking created a huge rift between the two. Although she did not want her second marriage to fail, her breaking point came when he physically manhandled Sarah and forced her out, locking her outside their home completely naked. She left with her three children.

Battered and emotionally broken, she hit a new low and her drinking worsened. She soon started dating another abusive man, who once waterboarded her in the kitchen sink. She had hit rock-bottom. She was in no condition to care for herself or her children. Her mental and emotional states were completely shattered. Her oldest child went to live with his dad, who provided a safe and loving environment for this sweet seven-year-old. Her two youngest children, four and five years old, went to live with caring people who wrapped them in a blanket of love, kindness, and safety.

At this point, Sarah did not see any purpose in living. Mum was still married to Peter and they both did their best to help, although Mum's *best* was not really the best. Mum would give Sarah more alcohol. She would add vodka to a pint of water and offer it to Sarah first thing in the morning in the hopes she could keep her hydrated and stop her from shaking. Peter, a light drinker, was beside himself with worry. He took Sarah to stay with our sister, Maria, who also did not drink, in the hope that she could help Sarah. Alas, Sarah was not going to stop. She went missing, staying with anyone who would accommodate her and her habit.

Nobody had notified me of how bad things had become for Sarah, and I had not had much communication with her during this time. That is, until I received a clear message from my spirit guides. They said: "Tracey, Sarah will be dead if you don't find and help her." I was taken aback, and immediately called Mum to ask her if she knew where Sarah was and if she was in any dire circumstance. Mum confessed everything that had been going on with Sarah and I revealed the message I was given by my guides. We both tried to track her down, to no avail. A week later, a taxi cab pulled up in Mum's driveway in the middle of the night with Sarah in the back seat, wearing only a stranger's jacket draped over her beaten and battered body. Peter paid the taxi fare and they wrapped her in a blanket and took her indoors. She weighed eighty-five pounds. She had been tied up, bitten all over her body, abused and thrown out on the street naked by some disgraceful, cowardly individuals.

Sarah then went to stay with Bernard, her dad's friend. He was a recovered alcoholic who was loving, patient and kind to Sarah because he understood what she was going through. I sensed it was the best place for her. I went to visit and she asked me to ask my spirit guides if she was going to die. Their reply was, "do you want to die, Sarah?"

She thought for a moment and replied, "I don't know if I can forgive myself for all of the hurt that I have created through my choices and actions. It's so scary to come into sobriety and look back at the person I had become in the grip of addiction. Part of me wants to stay in that dark place so that I don't have to look at it, but I really want to live." She paused, then continued, "so no. I don't want to die."

My guides then stated: "That is the answer to your question. With courage, hard work, and faith you can and will overcome your challenges and we will help you every step of the way." I worked with Sarah, giving her energy healing, and shortly after, she checked into rehab. The start of healing the cellular memory of her ancestral line had begun.

It has been almost twenty years and, guided by the help and loving touch of the Angels, she has not looked back. She has since become an accomplished holistic health practitioner, and a business owner, and is happily married to her husband, Kerbie. She is able to now help others heal, knowing that they are safe with her and will face no judgment or criticism from her as they go through their own healing journeys. I am incredibly proud of my baby sister. The strength and courage it took to overcome this period of her life is unfathomable. She saw the light shining on the first step of the ladder and climbed out of that dark pit, known as substance abuse, that so many feel they cannot. Let her story be an inspiration to anyone struggling with addiction: Life can be so much better when you have the courage to take the first step.

The Hummingbird

VIC AND I, WITH OLIVER AND LEWIS IN TOW, EMIGRATED FROM England to California in 2008. Our three-bedroom, second floor apartment was quite the healing space for us. Some people thought we were nuts or lost in grief to make such a huge change, especially in our forties. We knew it was the right thing to do. We always say that Clair is responsible for catapulting us over the Atlantic.

We had been settling into the American way of life for over a year when Vic had a bout of diverticulitis while away on a business trip in Canada. The ER doctors insisted that he needed to have an MRI scan to confirm the diagnosis. Vic reluctantly agreed. The scan not only confirmed diverticulitis, it highlighted a three-centimeter cancerous tumor encapsulated in his left kidney. A surgery to remove the mass was scheduled for January of 2010.

I had never felt so alone while sitting in the hospital waiting room, awaiting news from Vic's surgeon as his medical team worked to remove a chunk of Vic's kidney. My closest friends and family were thousands of miles away. I had done nothing but pray for help since his diagnosis and sitting there alone, I began to call in all of the healing Angels to assist him in his hour of need. I focused on seeing Vic and the entire medical team bathed in a beautiful golden light of positive healing energy to aid them in any way possible. After I had done that, I was left with the task of processing my own fears. I tried my best to remain positive. I felt myself slipping into deep sadness and fear of loss, and the emotional turmoil I had worked through after losing Clair weighed heavy on my heart once again.

As I waited for an update from the doctors regarding the progress of Vic's surgery, I was desperately trying to read a book I had picked up on a waiting room side table in a failed attempt to distract my mind. While gazing down at the open book in my hands, unable to get past the title, I sensed someone observing me. I looked up into the lovely face of a well-dressed elderly lady. She smiled and sat down beside me. She said, "is it your husband in surgery?"

I nodded my head, yes. She said, "is he a businessman?" She gently placed her hand on my arm. I confirmed this for the kind stranger. "He carries all the stress, sadness, and anger on the left side of his stomach." I had not told her why Vic was having surgery or which part of his body was being operated on. I sensed a tingling sensation in my heart that she had been sent by the Angels to help lift my spirit. In our short conversation she reassured me that all would be well, and then left as quickly as she had appeared. Her eloquent words, kindness, warmth, and confidence that everything would be well penetrated my vulnerable heart during our brief but insightful conversation. I felt much lighter during and after our connection. In only a few moments with this beautiful soul, I had been given a transmission of light full of courage, strength, and a huge dose of love in my moment of need.

Six hours had passed when the surgeon found me in the waiting room to let me know the procedure had gone well. I let out a huge sigh of relief and headed up to meet Vic in recovery.

Vic came out of surgery looking ghastly, his face a gray-green pallor. I must say, he looked terrible. I immediately put my hands over him to give him a boost of healing energy. He soaked everything I transmitted and more. So much, I nearly passed out! I had to sit down for at least thirty minutes to restore and recharge my own energy frequency.

The next day, while recovering, Vic told me he had heard Clair shout, "Oi, Dad!" This brought joy to our hearts and smiles to our faces, and some strength to get us through the next twelve months.

A year passed and it was time for Vic's annual checkup. He had already gone in for a scan and was scheduled to see his doctor to review the images. The day before his appointment, I was on my own, pottering around the apartment, when a tiny hummingbird flew in through the patio doors. I became concerned for the little chap. I said to the frightened bird, "it's okay, I won't harm you. We have to figure out a way to get you to safety." I asked my spirit guides to help me create a sacred energetic space while wrapping the little bird in the light of Unconditional Love, to keep him calm and make him feel secure. Simultaneously, Vic was walking up the stairs. When he reached the second level, he took off his jacket and placed his briefcase on the floor. He took in the scene and calmly walked over to my side. I said, "in a moment, I want you to outstretch your hand because I'm going to tell the little hummingbird to come down and sit on it. I've reassured him you will take him to safety."

Vic followed my instructions and gently raised his hand. The hummingbird flew towards Vic and landed on his extended finger. He slowly walked to the open patio door. I telepathically told the little bird to gather his strength before flying off. He did, allowing us to capture this special moment on camera. Afterwards, we sat talking about our special visitor when it dawned on me the symbolism for the hummingbird is joy. I am sure Clair had sent the little bird to alleviate her dad's stress, and to ensure that all would be well, and it was.

The hummingbird on Vic's finger.

Animal Visitors and Angels in Human Form

THE YEAR 2015 CAME UPON US SWIFTLY. VIC HAD SUFFERED A FEW severe bouts of diverticulitis. The most recent one left him hospitalized for a week and required another surgery. The day before he was admitted, we had a small bird tap on our front door. Our Angelic Loved Ones had sent another positive message via a feathered friend. The next morning, at 5:20 AM, we got in the car and headed out. I stopped at Starbucks to get myself a cup of tea and some snacks. I looked down at my receipt and noticed my change was $5.55. "555" is the number the Angels use to let me know they are present. I recognize the number as a positive sign. I smiled at the receipt and went over to the collection bar. Starbucks had only just opened and I had assumed I was alone in the coffee shop when, out of the corner of my eye, I saw an older gentleman saunter up beside me. I turned to look and he placed a full A4 piece of paper filled with blue ink smudges in my hand. He said, "would you read it?"

A little startled, I replied, "yes."

He had written a poem with verses full of peace, love, joy, positivity, and happiness. One line seemed to leap off the page: "Don't worry, all will be well," he had written, and next to the line he had drawn a large heart. I looked up into his unfamiliar eyes and recognized the soul.

I said, "this is absolutely beautiful and very helpful, thank you so much." He asked me if I would share his message and I replied, "yes, with the world." I turned to the coffee bar to pick up my drink and when I turned back to ask him a question, he was already gone. I left the coffee shop in quite a daze. I climbed into the car and announced, "we've just had a message not to worry, all will be well." This calming message was shown to be true. Vic's surgery to remove five inches of his colon took five hours and was successful. Vic came home to recuperate and within a day our small, feathered friend returned, this time, tapping on the window to say 'hello'.

Much like the mysterious and lovely elderly lady that comforted me in the waiting room during Vic's renal surgery, and who appeared to know far too much about our circumstances, I suspect the poet I encountered in the coffee shop was an angel in human form, wearing a human overcoat to assist and reassure Vic and I in a time of need. The easiest way for angels to work in this reality and around human people unnoticed is in human form. They typically appear from nowhere and disappear without a trace. Angels who appear in human form always emanate a deep sense of peace and have a sparkle of light, kindness, and love radiating from their eyes. They only take human form to be helpful, as messengers and servants of God, the Light, and their words are limited but profound.

My Angelic Friends have always taught me to respect and honor all life. They say if you talk to the animals, they will understand and communicate with you in whatever way they can.

My family always laughs when they see me asking a bee to leave our home. I have done this for many years and it works perfectly. I create a path of light to show these little black and yellow friends the way out. Then I ask them to leave, letting them know this indoor space is not good for them to be in. They fly out almost instantly.

Vic had an experience with the bees. We were outside with the family one evening and a bee landed on his leg. His first reaction was to swat the bee. Which he did a little too hard. The kids and I lovingly chastised him. Half-jokingly, I told him that this bee's friends would come back and sting him for treating their friend that way. He rolled his eyes and we continued our pleasant conversation. Within ten minutes of saying so, another bee entered our family circle and promptly stung Vic. Poor Vic did not get much sympathy. All he heard was our belly laughs and told-you-sos.

I do my best to look after the bees, they are dying off at an alarming rate. I have come to believe this is due to a loss of habitat and the increased use of environmental toxins and pesticides. They are such a gift to humanity. Bees are crucial to the growth of crops, helping to pollinate about one-third of the food we eat as humans and up to eighty percent of plants on earth. Because they are the main carriers of pollen between flowers, their role in helping those plants reproduce is essential. Flowering plants are a universal food source and the loss would be disastrous for almost every animal. We can help the bees by creating a small herb garden with basil, sage, mint, lemon balm, thyme, oregano, and rosemary. In doing so, we show our gratitude for the bees for the way they share with us. While my interactions with our animal and insect neighbors are primarily with birds, bees, and butterflies, I have also enjoyed my fair share of interactions with furrier creatures.

Lewis was in his senior year of high school and his girlfriend at the time had asked us to come to her last lacrosse game. Lewis, Vicky, my grandson, Ollie, and I met up with his girlfriend's family in the stadium and enjoyed the game together. At the end, our combined families were among the first ones to exit the stadium. As we were shuffling towards the exit gates, his girlfriend's relatives started to scream. A rat had run under her grandmother's wheelchair. They maneuvered the wheelchair backward and from about eight feet away, this cute baby rat looked up at me in absolute terror. All of the new foot-traffic must have confused him, causing him to be trapped out in the open. Forgetting where I was, I cried, "little rat, come to me and I will help you!" Instantly, the rat ran between my feet and gently placed its head on my foot. I asked the Angels to assist me in creating a beam of light directed towards the vacant bleachers at the back of the stadium. I pointed and told the little rat to run in the light to freedom. He made it about halfway to the bleachers when he veered off track. I shouted, "back in line!" He corrected his path and safely disappeared. I looked up to find Vicky laughing in amusement at what she had just seen. She said, "oh my goodness! You are a rat whisperer now?" Neither of us realized a crowd had formed behind us, we had all been blocking the exit. Goodness knows what the others thought. Hopefully, they were inspired to see rats for the intelligent and sentient beings they are.

Little bird visitors.

The Rainbow Heart Light

THE RAINBOW HEART LIGHT WAS ONE OF THE FIRST ENERGY images that revealed itself to me while in the USA. The visible manifestation of this energy, which has helped me heal tremendously, was caught on camera by a little handheld Canon. I experienced a calling in 2010 to attend a past-life regression certification course taught by Mary Elizabeth Raines in Sedona, Arizona. I was a little nervous about driving there, I had only been in the USA for a couple of years and it had taken me months to get used to tackling California's crazy traffic, at the same time, the urge to go was so strong, a new sense of confidence pulsed through my veins. My family, concerned for my safety and wellbeing, thought it would be wise for me to have a traveling companion. I agreed and put a call out to my spirit guides. I asked them for a beautiful soul to accompany me on the drive to Sedona. The next day, Mary Elizabeth called and asked if I would consider carpooling with a woman from Los Angeles. Alma Bella called me straightaway to introduce herself as my carpooling buddy and after a brief chat our travel plans were confirmed. I thanked the Angels for their prompt response to my prayer.

The day of our adventure soon arrived. I opened the door and recognized Alma immediately, not from this lifetime but from another. Our bond was instant: friends reunited. We chatted nonstop throughout the six-and-a-half-hour drive during which she revealed her name translates to beautiful soul in her native tongue. The Angels had not just arranged a traveling companion for me, they actually connected me with a beautiful soul by nature and by name.

When we arrived, we checked the area out and were honored to have witnessed a blessing ceremony being given by a Native American. We had our dinner and then retired to bed. I had been told by my spirit guides to have a room on my own. At about 2:00 AM, I realized why. For three hours my physical body was vibrating from the energy. I had a room full of souls chanting and taking me on what I can only describe as some kind of a vision quest. These souls were just pure light energy. I knew one of them in particular, but was not sure from where. I was told by these benevolent souls that I was being given the "Rainbow Light" as a gift. I certainly felt it—all my being was vibrating with the colors of the rainbow. I was also instructed to meditate the next morning on the Airport Mesa red rock we had previously witnessed being blessed and was told I would receive confirmation of the rainbow light I had been given.

Unable to go back to sleep, my head was spinning with questions and I felt supercharged with energy. I jumped out of bed, ate a light breakfast, and prepared myself for the day ahead. Alma and I had already planned to go back to the Airport Mesa to watch the sunrise. I was pondering on the message that I would "receive confirmation while on the red rock" and wondering how it would manifest when I heard my guide say: "ask your friend to take a photo of you with your camera while you meditate on the red rock." I then heard a gentle tap on the door and we headed out for the day.

We walked the short distance and climbed up the small incline and I took the opportunity to ask Alma to take some pictures of me while in meditation. Taking in the wonder of this sacred space I prepared for meditation. Still buzzing from my prior experience, I went into a gentle and calm state of being. Alma snapped a couple of pictures. We spent more time there and I took pictures of Alma and the surrounding area. Caught up in the moment we realized we needed to head to our course otherwise we would be late for our first day. While waiting to start the class I scrolled through the pictures. A rainbow light in the shape of a heart appeared to be approaching my hand. This was confirmation from the Great Spirit of everything that I had experienced and had been gifted with "The Rainbow Heart Light".

A few days into the past-life regression course, I was being regressed back by a PLR therapist into the life of a seven-year-old Native American girl, whose name was Tallulah, Choctaw for "running water" or "leaping water". Running Water, like my guardian Angel. Tallulah was a sparky little personality who was pleased with who she was and was especially proud of her grandfather, a well-respected spiritual medicine man. She adored him as he adored her. He was teaching her the ways of medicine and she was delighted that she would become a medicine woman of her tribe. Tallulah was a little older when she was taken from her grandfather and held captive so he would relinquish his power and silence his voice. Tallulah was beaten for speaking out to her captives about their injustice. In one of the beatings, they unintentionally killed her. During the soul review, the period when the soul has left the body and is reviewing key events and emotions of the life they had just experienced, there was a sense of disappointment that she had not fulfilled her destiny of becoming a spiritual medicine woman. She felt it was her actions of standing up for herself against her captives that had gotten her killed. It dawned on me that I had brought this fear into my present life. I did not speak until I was three years old. I always had great difficulties speaking out and standing up for myself during my younger years. It was a challenge I had to overcome. After having this past life and others of a similar nature, I had never healed myself fully up to this point. On the physical level, I had regularly suffered from sore throats, issues with my teeth, and even had a recurring cyst for many years on my inner lip. I do believe all of this came about from the fear of standing up for myself and speaking out.

During this past life regression, I recognized one of the souls who had been with me through my vision quest on my first night in Sedona, as being my grandfather in this life of Tallulah. I am still amazed at the intensity of the energy I experienced through my vision quest. I felt like every part of my physical body had been healed and cleansed. After revisiting the life of Tallulah, I had another energetic experience once back at my room. Once again, I was awakened in the middle of the night when my hands started vibrating. I felt they were ten times bigger and filled with this remarkable rainbow light. I then visualized this healing energy radiating out to every corner of the world. I also knew that my body had undergone another deep cleanse, an energetic cleanse, from everything I had ever experienced in this life and prior ones. The infusion of pure light was to expedite my own healing journey and give me a great foundation to clear the rest of the residue cellular memory that needed to be released.

The Angels and my guides shared this message regarding this energy: *The Rainbow Heart Light is a gift from the Creator for all beings in every dimension. The Rainbow Heart Light energy brings healing, love, and compassion to all life. Rainbow Heart Light energy helps us to release fear and encourages us to forgive all, opening our hearts to unconditional love, truth, and wisdom. This energy will be shared with many in their time of need.*

Eighteen months later, my first biological grandson was born. I lovingly call him Ollie-Bear. He is quite a special soul who came into this life with a few physical challenges. He was born with a critical congenital heart defect known as Tetralogy of Fallot. In simple terms he was born with four heart defects which meant he would need surgeries to patch and replace parts of his heart throughout his life.

His first open-heart surgery was at the tender age of three and a half months old. The surgery went well and Vicky decided that she was strong enough to stay the night alone in the hospital with Ollie. She sent us home to get some rest and sleep, knowing we would be back early in the morning to help her. Vic, Oliver, and I woke up the next morning to half a dozen missed calls and voicemails that Vicky had left starting around 3:00 AM and every hour after, saying that Ollie experienced a junctional ectopic tachycardia (JET) and then flatlined. She let us know how the doctors and nurses filled the room to perform compressions on his tiny chest and torso and revived him. After confirming with her that Ollie was stable, we headed back to the hospital immediately. Oliver beat me there. As I was entering the intensive care unit, a nurse blocked my path and asked me to wait outside the room. A deep inner panic began to wash over me. Not only did I feel my own fear rising, but I also felt the fear coming from my son and daughter-in-law's hearts as Ollie was receiving compressions for a second time. He had experienced a second JET in only a few hours and flatlined once more. I needed to get into the room to bring energy to Ollie in his moment of need. I silently asked my spirit guides and Angels to help. The lady who had been stopping me from going changed her stance and said, "go they need you".

On entering the room, Ollie's twelve-pound body was surrounded by doctors and nurses tending to his needs. I put my arms around the kids and asked them to join me in sending a beautiful pink light filled with unconditional love and positive healing energy to aid Ollie and the doctors and nurses helping him. Within seconds of doing this he was revived and began to stabilize. I silently thanked God and all of our Angelic Friends and of course the medical team. I knew in that instant all would be well.

A few hours later, Vicky and I sat quietly talking while Ollie slept when she suddenly blurted out, "Tracey is he going to live?"

Without hesitation I replied, "yes, he's here to stay. He has a lot of work to do. He's here to make people smile." As soon as I finished speaking, the electric motion paper towel dispenser across the room started spewing paper towels everywhere. The nurse, sitting at her station, looked rather unnerved as there was nobody on that side of the room. We smiled knowing it was a confirmation from loved ones in spirit. I had already sensed Ollie's

Aunty Clair was with us, helping as much as she could, and also the spirit of our dear friend's daughter, who had been an ER nurse when in the physical.

Another nurse came in to check on Vicky, to see how she was holding up after the long day we all had. She said, "how are you doing, momma?"

Before Vicky could answer, a young resident doctor butted in and said, "oh, she's fine, she slept through the whole thing this morning," referring to the first JET in the early hours.

Vicky became speechless and after the resident left, she said, "I wasn't asleep for a second. I was watching from behind the curtain. I just didn't want them to see me and worry about me. I knew one of them would walk over to me to comfort me and I didn't want them to. I was there the whole time watching and praying but I didn't want to distract any of them." She hung her head in shame, wondering what they must have been thinking of her after the horrible night and day she had. "I even told them before they began removing his pacemaker the second time. I was watching his numbers and I warned them he was repeating the same numbers he had before his first JET. They didn't believe me when I went to get them." Vicky had been watching Ollie's monitor nonstop from when he was admitted into the recovery. She updated us frequently and she had told us before the second crash that she told the nurse his numbers were off.

As I have said before, words carry energy. While some words can empower others, some words can add to the burden another is already carrying.

A year to the day after Ollie's surgery, I woke up with a children's story. I ran downstairs and asked Vicky to grab a pen and paper. She then proceeded to write the story down word for word. The Angels said that I would meet another heart-centered beautiful soul to do the illustrations. We waited patiently for five months when a friend asked if I still needed an illustrator. She passed my details onto her friend and a few days later I received an email from Sherae. I opened it and instantly felt the love from her heart. I shouted to Vicky, "she's here!"

I knew Sherae was the one the Angels had told me about. We quickly arranged a meeting. When the day came for us to meet, I opened my front door and we stood there looking at one another. Tears filled our eyes. We knew each other not from this lifetime but from many before—soul-sisters in the highest sense. Sherae is a special person and she embodies creativity. She is pure of heart and loves unconditionally. I am blessed to call her my soul-sister and to have her as my friend. She is incredibly creative, channeling light into all her amazing heart-work and pouring love into the world.

Not long after, "Ollie Bear's Adventures with the Rainbow Heart Light" was born. The Angels brought forth these little books filled with love and tools for the imagination to assist children in their moments of need; to teach them the skill of meditation, so they can be centered and filled with peace and hope throughout their plights.

Ollie and the Violet Flame

In August of 2016 we found out that Ollie's heart had enlarged. It was overcompensating for his defective pulmonary valve which forced the heart muscles to work harder. After consulting the cardiologist, Ollie's pediatrician explained that although he was a small four-year-old, his heart was closer in size to that of a ten-year-old. He asked us to imagine throwing a bucket of water up at a tube, saying that while some of the water would get in, much of it would splash back down and it would take much more effort to get the necessary amount of water through that tube. Similarly, Ollie's heart had to pump more often to make up for the blood that was not making it through the pulmonary valve. His second open-heart surgery was scheduled for November that same year.

Vicky had scheduled a meeting with a well-known local spiritual advisor and medium for some clarity and reassurance on the issue. The guidance she received was helpful, but most interesting to Vicky, was the theme of Saint Germain and the Violet Flame. The intuitive passed a message to Vicky from her guides to tell her that the message of the Violet Flame was significant in Ollie's life. Vicky shared the message with Oliver and I and we pondered the meaning together for some time.

The last week in October was quickly upon us and we had been trying to distract our minds. Vicky, Ollie and I had plans to go to our local HomeGoods store for Halloween decorations. Before we left, I caught up with Barbara over Skype. During our conversation, her spirit guides interrupted with a message.

Barbara relayed the message from her guides: "Tracey will find something special on the floor. This is a gift to help during these challenging times."

We assumed I would actually find something on the floor. I said goodbye to Barbara and drove to HomeGoods. Cruising around the store I saw a crystal on the shelf and standing near it was an employee. I said, "this is a lovely piece."

She spontaneously said, "that's nothing, have you seen the one on the floor? Come with me, I will show you." My heart started pounding as Barbara's message rang in my ears. At a fast pace I excitedly followed her. Right before my eyes, standing on the floor, was a three-and-a-half-foot tall amethyst cathedral with a low price. I happily purchased this huge crystal gift, knowing it was meant to help Ollie. When we returned home, Ollie was so excited to watch Oliver place it for us in the house. He smiled and gave it big hugs each time he passed by it. What a beautiful gift we found on the floor.

There are many metaphysical properties to amethyst. It dissolves negativity, alleviates sadness and fear, and brings balance and harmony to anyone or any space. The crystal is shaped like a flame. I likened it to the violet flame. The violet flame carries a unique spiritual energy which is known to help overcome emotional and physical problems; it is the flame of forgiveness, purifying and transmuting negative energy. I often use violet light to cleanse and disperse negativity, replacing the energy with love, healing, and protection. I became aware of the violet flame and the Bodhisattva Kwan Yin in the early 1990's while attending a workshop to become a Magnified Healing practitioner. A Bodhisattva is a person who has achieved enlightenment but chose to forgo Nirvana and instead assist humanity. In 2014, I received a message from a beautiful heart-centered intuitive. She told me that I had resided and worked in the temples of Kwan Yin in a previous lifetime. The spark of recognition came like a blast of light in my mind's eye, giving me the gift of clarity. As I was bathed in the divine light of Kwan Yin's love, I remembered the bond that had been created in my prior life and my heart filled with an abundance of love for her.

Kwan Yin is the Bodhisattva of Compassion. She blesses us with healing, love, and understanding. Many have said she maintained life in the physical form for one thousand years before ascending, retaining a deep love for humanity. Kwan Yin was the original Keeper of the Violet Flame for two thousand years until Saint Germain succeeded her. Saint Germain is an ascended master whose mission is to bring awareness of God's sacred violet light into the consciousness of humanity. The male and female energy contained within the sacred flame is now perfectly balanced, creating a powerful gift to aid humanity in transmuting negativity.

About a year earlier, Vicky and I drove to the visiting Gemfaire in Costa Mesa. The plan was to pick up a few heart-shaped crystals. We first stopped at the booth of one of our favorite vendors to greet him and while browsing his assorted collection of crystals and minerals strewn over the stall, a sparkle of light radiating off of a piece of quartz crystal caught my eye just as I looked up. My spirit guides gave me a nudge to ask about the quartz crystal figure. I could not make out the form, but knew I needed to ask the seller what it was and if it was for sale. I stood in line patiently waiting for my turn. I was not at all concerned if someone before me wanted to purchase it. I knew it was meant for me. While waiting, Vicky sauntered up. I asked her if she could see the quartz crystal and if she could make out what it was.

"It looks like Kwan Yin," she said. The seller, now free to speak to me, confirmed this, brought her down from the shelf, and placed her in my hands. I was astonished by the masterful piece of artwork. The seller had been the keeper of this majestic piece for many years and until now had no intention of selling it. The detail was superlative. Kwan Yin had been hand-carved from one piece of clear quartz by a member of a small group of Chinese artisans. The seller was now ready to release her to a good home. I bought her and promised I would cherish her.

She sits pride of place in-front of a large smoky quartz point and other special crystal treasures.

In February of 2020, I had followed Vic into our bedroom, chatting about the day's events, when I noticed the image of Kwan Yin manifesting in the smoky quartz crystal. I could not believe my eyes and still have difficulty describing the phenomenon. Kwan Yin's image was not reflected, but duplicated, more like seeing the much smaller negative of a photograph in the smokey quartz in comparison to the large Kwan Yin quartz carving. Kwan Yin's image was reproduced and outlined in light, exactly the same, down to the beads around her neck. The Kwan Yin carved from quartz was facing away from the smokey quartz crystal.

I called Vic over to show him. "Oh fuck!" he said, "That's really clear, what does it represent?" I could not be sure of its meaning, I felt it was only a blessing.

Vicky said to me after seeing the photograph I took of it, "I think it's a confirmation for you. Any of us can go out and find a figure or image of Kwan Yin and bring it home, but here she chose to show herself to you to say: Yes, I am with you."

And I heard clearly from the Angels, "yes, that's true."

While contemplating this message it dawned on me why Kwan Yin had chosen this time to manifest. Vic had offered to let Oliver and Vicky and their boys move back in with us to conserve their resources while Oliver worked and returned to college. By March 2020, the four of them had managed to move out of their condo and into our house just in time for the stay-home order. Many countries had imposed lockdowns to stop the spread of the coronavirus, Covid-19. Intense energies of fear, shock, anger, helplessness, manipulation, and loss consumed the Western World. The pandemic has caused so much uncertainty and many people went into a tailspin of negativity. Some of the expectations for human behavior from what was being called "the new normal", included: only leaving one's house to collect essentials; only leaving one's home to exercise if a six-foot distance was maintained from all other people; only indoor businesses deemed "essential" could continue to operate; and under no circumstances was anyone to visit family or friends in this time and absolutely no indoor dining. Many had been let go from their jobs or lost the businesses they had built in a matter of weeks. The morale of the collective population, facing threats of financial instability or ruin and fears of sickness and death for themselves or loved ones, had hit a low. Feelings of disaster loomed in the air, and suspicion and unneighborly conduct surfaced, heightening the sense of insecurity and vulnerability. Stockpiling of all things occurred, from food and medicine to toilet rolls and antibacterial wipes, due to sudden fear of having to go without.

All this being said, it shows just how fragile the world we have created really is. My guides have told me that this was a time of observation, mindfulness, self-reflection, and meditation in preparation for action. Teetering on just the idea of economic collapse, we have asked ourselves: has this been brought on through the energy of greed? Collectively, we are realizing that it was time spent together, not material goods, which brought us the greatest joy. While fearing the loss of our creature comforts, we were all beginning to ask: how many of those items being stockpiled do others in less developed areas go without on a day-to-day basis? While watching the Covid-19 infection rate on the television every day, many began to wonder: where were the numbers of those facing starvation around the world due to the newly imposed lockdowns, or those who would have starved in those months anyway? And when the schools were shut, it dawned on so many for the first time to ask: where were the solutions for the children who were removed from the institutions that kept them fed and safe throughout the day, who were now stuck at home with those who neglect and abuse them?

When faced with adversity, we have to remain calm and remember to support one another on a practical level as best we can, with all things considered. After debriefing with my friend, Sherae, she reminded me that this is the return of Christ Consciousness energy, or the energy of Christ's love for humanity, and Kwan Yin carries this magnificent frequency with her. Sherae sensed this energy revealed itself to me so I can feel reassured in turn radiating Kwan Yin's love and to reassure others with this amazing confirmation. Kwan Yin has heard our call in our time of need; her love for humanity, carried her from beyond the veil, bestowing the world with her light and dispersing negativity to remind us that this too shall pass.

Most recently during readings, the Angels have been sharing a consistent message.

Message from the Angels:

You have been a weary warrior on life's path. You are being pushed and pulled in many directions, creating inner turmoil and burdening your already overloaded emotions. Humanity's collective fog of fear is hanging around in the atmosphere, being sucked up by many who are already conflicted. These negative emotions are everything humanity is releasing during this time of transition. There is a huge cleansing on a mass scale of humanity's cellular memory of injustice, victimization, anger, fear, and frustration. Cellular memory cannot be healed while there are so many negative emotions being released from individuals. We are calling on you all to be the Beacons of Light to help transmute this energy. We are sending a Golden Light down through your crown chakra, permeating every cell of your being, thus releasing the emotions you have all been collecting together as a human race and helping you clear and release your own personal conflicts at the same time. We are now strengthening your connection to source energy, healing and filling you with strength to aid on the path you walk. You will feel better within your heart and on every level. You have to remain neutral and objective. In other words, stay off the battlefield. We are not asking you to silence your voice, we are asking you to recognize that the higher level of consciousness that your soul emits is the energy of truth that speaks for itself. Staying neutral means that the truth emanates from your energy field and radiates outwards into the world without engaging in the negativity created when you participate in a fight. Despite good intentions, the fighting creates so much more division. If you say "you are" and "I am", or "us" and "them", an energetic separation is created.

If we say "we are" the energy of unification is created for humanity. This energy is all-inclusive, regardless of color, creed, religion, social status, or political affiliation.

When you hold this intention, you instantly become a Beacon of Light, standing with millions of light workers side-by-side, with all of your loving ancestral line in spirit behind you, the Ascended Masters with you, and we, the Angels, all channeling God's light together as one, through our hearts and through the hearts of every being, including yours because you are the physical anchor of light in this reality. Together we shine the light of love in all parts of the world to illuminate truth and transmute negativity. Never doubt the power of LOVE, it is a formidable force. Every light worker who has incarnated at this time has been chosen to be here because they can hold the light and not succumb to the shadow. This is your purpose, to shine light and be light.

Now back to Ollie's story:

Ollie was four years old when he was scheduled for his second open-heart surgery. We had taught him to envision the healing colors of light energy to help him manage any emotional and physical discomfort. His favorite color to use was green.

Ollie had chosen a clear quartz crystal heart to give to Dr Starr at his pre-op appointment. He described it to her as a Golden Heart Light, she thanked him and popped it into her shirt pocket and told him she would keep it close to her heart during his surgery and all the special children she would treat thereafter. While this exchange took place the room was filled with a soothing light of Unconditional Love.

November the 9th, 2016, was a big day for America. Many were waking in the early hours to the news of who would be president of the United States for the next four years. This was the furthest thing from our thoughts. We were all up by 6:00 AM, busily preparing to go to CHOC, Children's Hospital of Orange County. While sitting on the settee in our home waiting to leave, I reached into my purse to retrieve my phone. I was about to send a text when I heard the sound of a notification ping alerting me to an incoming message. It was from John St. Julien. John is the founder of Feathers Tale Children's Village in Kilimanjaro, Tanzania. He has dedicated his life to make the world a better place for many underprivileged children and their families. Vic and I had fully sponsored two little boys, Jafeth and Calvin, for the past few years.

With a puzzled expression on my face, I opened up the message and began to read: "Hi Tracey, hope you and the family are doing well. There is no easy way to tell you this, so I will just have to come out and say it. Sadly, little Jafeth has passed away, he was swimming with his friends, and there was some sort of accident, perhaps the current of the river, we don't know. He passed away under the water. We are all heartbroken here, he was a wonderful young man with so much ahead of him. But I guess he's in a better place now. We are just praying for his family now. Yours in love, light, and sorrow, John."

Heartbroken, I did not share this news with the others. I silently prayed and sent an abundance of loving healing light to Jafeth's sweet soul, for his family, and the other children who would be grieving his loss, without tipping off Vicky and Oliver about the devastating news. Somehow, with the help of the Angels and their healing light placed over my shoulders like a blanket I swallowed my tears, gathered my strength, and kept the knowledge within. I consoled myself with the fact that Jafeth was now in God's embrace.

Ollie's surgery was successful and had finished two and a half hours earlier than expected. Dr. Starr greeted us in the waiting area with the fantastic news. We thanked the medical staff and the Angels. Before she left, she pulled the heart crystal from her top pocket and knowingly smiled at us. Ollie's healing process was rapid. He walked on his own less than 48-hours after the surgery, greeted everyone with a smile, and was determined to complete any task the nurses gave him. Ollie had been seeing a hyperbaric oxygen therapist that Sherae referred us to in Mission Viejo, Mark Westaway, who provided him with care before and after the surgery to prevent infection and promote healing.

In addition to incorporating hyperbaric oxygen therapy, healthy eating, exercise, fresh air, and sunshine into Ollie's wellness routine, we had taught him to use breathing and visualization techniques. We witnessed him using these breathing techniques and visualization to help him deal with his discomfort. When the nurse asked him what he was doing, he explained that he was filling the room with green heart light. He told them how it made him feel better, saying that it worked like magic. He gently moved his hands in a wave motion to demonstrate the unseen flow of energy. She was quite astonished as she continued removing the tubes that were draining excess fluids from openings in his chest.

Not even his cardiologist was prepared for how quickly he recovered. He came home from the hospital within four days of being admitted. When he had met all of the requirements to leave, Vicky and Oliver sent us home while they received discharge instructions and picked up his medication from the pharmacy. While waiting for their return, A friend and I were chatting in the kitchen at my house, when we heard loud childlike giggles and footsteps running up the stairs in excitement. We gaped at each other.

"Who was that?" my friend asked, "it's only the two of us here, shall I go and check for intruders?"

I knew this was no earthly person. I told her not to worry as I sensed it was a happy soul visiting us from the spirit world. Two minutes later, Oliver, Vicky and Ollie returned from the hospital. The house went quiet.

Over the next couple of days, we all heard more paranormal activity around the house. I had been waiting for the spirit to reveal themselves. I sensed that this was a friendly child and I wondered whether it could be Jafeth. Alas, there was too much going on in my personal life to gain clarity from my intuitive side, so I called my dear friend Barbara to give her an update on Ollie and to ask her opinion on the new presence in our home. I informed her I had sensed a happy soul and I told her I felt it was a child.

"I feel this soul is a child and that this is a little boy from Africa," she said. Barbara was unaware of our connection to John St. Julien, and she did not know anything about Jafeth or what had just happened. After she said that I felt goosebumps. She went on to say, "he has come to visit Ollie to see how he was living in another part of the world," and explained that he wanted to visit and be a part of our family for a short time so he could help us out. My heart burst with love for this beautiful soul. Barbara went on to say, "he's very happy and it's an absolute joy for me to share this news with you."

I got the impression that Jafeth wanted to help our family in our time of need. Whatever the reason, we give love and thanks to our helpful friend. I never felt Jafeth was lost; it was his soul's choice with the help of the Angels to have this experience with us before he left this earthly realm.

One week after surgery, Ollie's right atrial hypertrophy had reversed. His cardiologist said he had never seen this happen this quickly before. The full understanding of the gift I received on the airport Mesa hit me in that moment. It showed me by standing together in the light of love and positivity, we can create miracles.

Our family is in deep gratitude to our Angelic Friends, all of the wonderful doctors, nurses, and everyone who sent their love thoughts, prayers and light. Ollie has yearly cardiology checkups. As he grows, the pulmonary valve will once again need replacing and we are not sure how many surgeries he will need in the future. For now, we are just enjoying life with him.

Ollie hugging the amethyst crystal.

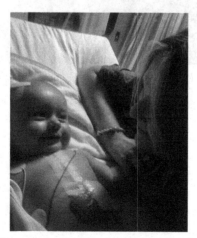

Ollie recovering from his first open heart surgery.

Image of Kwan Yin appearing in the smokey quartz crystal.

Mateo Lewis

WHILE LEWIS WAS IN BOOT CAMP, VICKY AND OLIVER DISCOVERED that after six years of being a family of three, she was pregnant with their second child. Due to the possible genetic component related to Tetralogy of Fallot, Vicky agreed to see a perinatal specialist in conjunction with her regular obstetrician. She wanted to be sure that they were prepared this time and if there were any abnormalities. In the case there was, she would not attempt a natural birth, as they had with Ollie, which unknowingly caused their newborn so much distress. Instead, she would agree to another cesarean. Two ultrasounds performed by the perinatologist eased their concerns, but not because of the medical nature of the exams or the expertise of the doctor—Ollie's condition had not been detected by any scans or tests performed during her pregnancy with him—no, what we saw on these ultrasound images were reassuring for reasons personal to us. One of the printed ultrasound stills had the image of an Angel watching over the small body and the second had a little heart light appearing on the baby's leg. During the same scan, Victoria was told the sex of her baby, a boy. While they had already discussed the name Mateo for their next son, upon realizing that he would be a father again to a little boy with the same seven-year age difference as he had with his own younger brother, Oliver was adamant that his middle name would be Lewis. This was a nice surprise to all of us, especially Lewis, who took this special honoring to heart. Oliver is not an overtly sentimental person.

Mateo Lewis was born on the 20th of May, 2019. After a difficult pregnancy and a lot of preparation, Oliver and Vicky were hoping to have a natural birth. Alas, this was not to be.

Vicky's water had broken sometime after her due date, but not enough for her to recognize the event and labor never started. At her next OB check-up, she failed her stress test and her ultrasound showed that her amniotic fluid was measuring low. Subsequently, a cesarean section was scheduled to take place that evening. Vicky's mum, Jill, and I received text messages from Vicky immediately following her appointment to update us on the planned arrival of our grandson, and to prepare us for the support she and Oliver would need during and following the surgery. She then calmly called her mum, Jill, on the phone to ask her to be in the operating room with her and called me to ask me to support Oliver, who she knew would be beside himself with worry while she was in there. Vicky did not ask Oliver to be in the operating room, in full knowledge that the sight of blood alone and the thought of her being cut open was enough to make Oliver dizzy; he had to be wheeled out of the theater during Ollie's birth. Jill left her work early and made the nearly one-hundred-mile drive south believing that she had plenty of time to make it to the surgery, which was scheduled for 6:20 PM.

At around 4:00 PM, while waiting patiently at home, wondering what time I should leave, I heard my guides say, "Tracey go now." The urge was incredibly strong. I kissed Vic and Ollie goodbye and told them, "I need to go now."

Vic asked "what's the rush? You have plenty of time."

"I don't know," I replied, "they must need me there for some reason or another."

I arrived at the hospital at 4:20 PM. In the room, I was goofing around to distract Vicky and Oliver's minds, thinking that I was there to ease their worries, when the nurse came in and said they had moved Vicky's surgery time up.

She said, "we'll be taking you back in the next forty-five minutes or so." We all looked at the clock and knew that Jill would not be able to make it to the hospital in time. I felt sad for

Jill, I knew she wanted to be there to support Vicky in any way she could.

I said, "don't worry, I will go in with you." Vicky sighed with relief. The next thing I knew I was all kitted out in scrubs. I had been wearing open-toed sandals, not the best footwear for the operating theater, so Vicky offered up her black flat shoes, laughing about the fact that they would be two sizes too big for me. I promptly put the oversized shoes on and started doing a penguin impression. The laughter lightened the situation. Laughter truly is the best medicine. I was so nervous on entering the surgical room. Reciting to myself, "you are brave, be brave, you can do this."

Vicky had chosen a collection of ABBA songs to be played during surgery. I did my best to reassure Vicky by stroking her head while administering healing energy to her the whole time, making sure she was comfortable. Vicky said this helped her especially when she felt more than just the normal tugging as the surgeon sliced through, cutting out and discarding layers of scar tissue and flesh. The ABBA song "SOS" rang in my ears during this moment. I called in the Angels to help alleviate Vicky's discomfort as she started shaking. Mateo was pulled from Vicky's womb at 6:02 PM, weighing seven pounds and nine ounces. The nurse called me over to meet him and asked me if I would like to cut the umbilical cord. In a daze I nodded yes. She handed me the scissors and as I cut the cord, I heard one of my guides say, "you were there to witness the death, now welcome him to his rebirth".

As I welcomed this sweet soul into the family fold, I pondered on what these words meant. My heart was bursting with love as I held my new grandbaby. The nurse and I then took him over to his mum. Vicky, still shaking and trying to calm her breath, had tears of love rolling down her face while gazing at her beautiful baby boy. Witnessing the love between Vicky and Mateo was precious. I felt honored and blessed to be a part of such a wonderful gift. In a dreamy state, I headed out to swap with Oliver, who was filled with joy and pride on meeting his newborn son.

I went to the waiting area to locate Jill and Oren, Vicky's dad, to tell them the good news. While guzzling water and trying to calm myself, I took in everything I had just witnessed. Not every day does one see the open insides and organs of their daughter-in-law. I realized in that moment that even though Jill has always been such a strong woman, it would have been painful for her to see her child in so much fear and discomfort. The Angels had intervened and planned everything out for the highest good of our souls. They always know best. Vic arrived with Ollie and we all chatted happily in anticipation of introducing Ollie to the newest member of our family, Mateo. While I am still unclear about the message I received from my guide, I have trust that all will be revealed to me according to divine time.

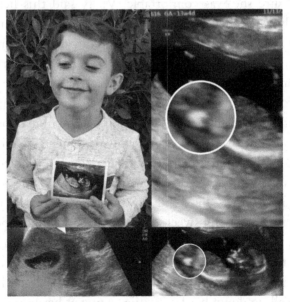

Ollie holding ultrasound images of Mateo.

Healing the Cellular Memory

WE ALL HAVE AN ENERGETIC MEMORY STORED WITHIN OUR DNA, genetic information which every cell is created from. This aggregation of the energetic memories of each cell is metaphysically known as the subconscious. While there is still much to be discovered about the subconscious, from a metaphysical perspective this term refers to all motivating factors, emotions, phobias, epiphanies, Deja vu, knowing and remembrance that cannot be logically explained by events experienced by the conscious mind. It is to my understanding through the wisdom of our Angelic Friends that generational emotions and trauma-based patterns manifest through what is referred to as the cellular memory. Separate from physical influence and individual experience, there is also a cellular memory and soul remembrance of one's own past lives which influences the soul during a new physical experience. Cellular memory is not limited to only negative family patterns but also embodies positive qualities and skill sets, as well.

Even those with wonderful childhoods can still have traumatic cellular memories from prior lifetimes or ones passed down from generation to generation. In other words, the cellular recollections that are affecting a person may not even belong to them. When triggered, these memories can manifest as feelings of inadequacy, anger, fear, sadness, and anxiety. They may be set off by a thoughtless comment, event, or even our own sabotaging thoughts, consequently creating more limiting belief systems. We have a tendency to think it is our present circumstance that can stir so much inner unrest, when in fact it is usually the cellular memory of emotional pain from the past which causes much of our inner turmoil. When you have the same thoughts or emotions automatically triggered by a certain event, the same cellular memory is activated and you are not usually aware of where it came from and why you feel the way you do.

For example, the cellular memory of inadequacy which many of us have a strong sense of. Do you feel good enough? Do you feel smart enough? Are you attractive enough? These doubts can arise often, even when asked to go and meet a new group of people, have you turned down an invitation because of these feelings? Are these fears based on any logic? Why would you feel this way? Obviously, you have never met these people. They are no more or less than you. They are just souls experiencing a different journey. Always remember, some will like you, love you, or sometimes not. It is not personal; we are all different energy frequencies. The ones we do not gel with are not meant to be around us, or are only meant to be around for a short time. Like oil and water: you can shake them up together and they will blend for a short time, but they will always separate from each other again. If you look on it as protection instead of rejection it instantly alleviates the feelings of inadequacy.

When the cellular memory of inadequacy is triggered, it may be due to experiencing many lifetimes of not achieving your goals or overcoming your obstacles. It can also be due to feelings of rejection from loved ones or society, hence the reluctance to meet new people, logically knowing this feeling is silly and unjustified, but still feeling a deep conflict within.

One of my own cellular memories I am working to overcome is the fear of being seen or speaking out, even in a small group of people, my heart would palpitate. I would feel like I could not breathe or speak, no matter how ridiculous this sounded, or how much I wanted to speak up, the overwhelming cellular memory of fear would create a restriction in my voice box and I would end up fumbling over my words. I understand where this cellular memory of fear started. I have had many lifetimes where I was not treated nicely for voicing my opinion. This left me with not only a deep sense of fear, but also the energy of keep-quiet-and-coast-along-without-being-noticed for the sake of self-preservation. Although it is still a work in progress, I will overcome and heal this cellular memory in this lifetime.

Another example: One of my clients had been having difficulty conceiving. She and her husband had tried for many years to no avail. During her session, I was shown one of her past lives relevant to her current situation of infertility. This healthy young lady before me had experienced a horrendous time in her prior incarnation. She was extremely young, homeless, pregnant, and alone. The forlorn young girl had to give birth on her own in the middle of a field. Dread filled her heart and soul as she desperately tried to bring her baby into the world. Alas, this was not meant to be and her baby passed away in her arms. Shortly after, she transitioned, too. The shock from this experience created a deep fear regarding pregnancy and birth. The cellular memory of fear was triggered by a desire for a baby in this lifetime and subconsciously blocked the physical pregnancy from happening. The Angels told me that the energetic block was coming from the past and this would not happen again in this lifetime. I gave her this message and we both sent healing light with the help of the Angels to heal the cellular memory. A few months later she became pregnant. She is now the proud mother to a beautiful baby girl.

The belief systems created in the present incarnation are developed and embellished through repeated experiences in our early years, and are typically based on our environment and the perceptions of our parents, teachers, and religious figures. Our perceptions are also influenced by social institutions, media, music, and literature. You may even perceive some beliefs as fact. We have to free our minds from negative beliefs to help heal the cellular memories. Remember that thoughts create energy, and negative thoughts add to an already overloaded cellular memory. We can also project the very thing we fear. Once we are able to be free minded, we gain a new sense of wonder without limitation, which is an important factor for our peace of mind and quest for spiritual growth.

Examples of Created Beliefs

1. Thoughtless Comment: In childhood you might have overheard an adult conversation comparing you to a sibling, along the lines of, "my son is so musical and creative, but my daughter is tone deaf. It is a shame she is not at all musical." Overhearing the negative comment about your lack of musical ability may cause you to automatically create the belief system that you are not musically inclined because you are tone deaf, thus, never attempting to pick up a musical instrument.

    Changing the Belief: Once you realize that this statement by a parent is an opinion and not truth, you can begin to awaken the seed of creativity that is dormant within you. Change this belief by acknowledging that you are musical, we all are. If you choose to, you will learn music and can then see what your musical edge may be. This process is not about perfection, it is just about enjoying the adventure of awakening your innate creativity.

2. Intentional Put-Downs: Your brother frequently tells you that you are ugly and fat and that no one will love you, creating the core belief you are not lovable, you are ugly, and fat so no one can love you.

    Changing the Belief: Once you realize that your brother's statement that you are ugly and fat is not true, it was just a way to hurt you due to his own inner fears and insecurities, you can begin to change this belief by reaffirming that you are beautiful, inside and out, we all are. You chose this perfect body to have the most wonderful adventure in this incarnation, and you are deserving of love. You are loved, we are loved, we all see the beauty in each other.

3. Self-sabotage: You believe the world is filled with negative energy which will sabotage your own happiness and nothing good can happen to you.

    Changing the Belief: Once you realize that viewing the world through negative eyes attracts the energy of the things you fear, and sabotages the joy in your life, you overcome a common belief. Your new belief is that the world is filled with positive energy and many beautiful things that I can love, cherish, and enjoy, without fear of negativity.

Healing the Cellular Memory and Changing False Belief Systems

MANY YEARS AGO, A YOUNG LADY, WENDY, CAME TO SEE ME FOR a reading. She was in the process of fertility treatment after trying to conceive naturally for ten years. During the session, I was intuitively shown she had been sexually abused. She confirmed this was true. My spirit guides told me that because of this experience, a false belief system had been created, which blocked the energy of conception. This was partly influenced by some misinformed opinion from an acquaintance who had told her that because she was abused, she would become an abuser. Tears ran down her face as she confirmed this was her deepest fear. The Angels and I reassured her this was not true. It was someone else's belief system that she had added to her own. I asked her to come back and see me directly after having her eggs transferred to her womb. She did and while I held my hands over her, acting as a conduit for the divine healing light of Unconditional Love and positive healing energy to shine through, I heard my spirit guide, Professor Bob, clearly say, "all three eggs will stay".

I shared this message from Professor Bob and we laughed together, and after a few moments, she said, "does that mean I am having triplets?"

My mouth dropped open involuntarily, and I blurted out, "yes, and you will have more babies, naturally." We burst into fits of giggles. Professor Bob had spoken. All we had to do now was wait and see. Wendy gave birth to triplets eight months later. Then had two more babies conceived without fertility treatments.

The removal of the false belief and healing of the cellular memory was all that she needed to do to become the amazing mother of five that she is today.

Wendy also found the profound strength within her to take her abuser to court. He was sentenced to fourteen years for rape, assault, and battery.

Healing emotional wounds at the cellular level and clearing limiting core belief systems is easier than you think, thanks to the advice and tools given to us from our Angelic Friends. All we have to do is recognize when a cellular memory has been triggered and use the exercise below to clear them, thus, healing the past, present, and future. The energetic Pink Light given to us by the Angels is a powerful tool in healing the cellular memory, changing the way we experience events. Use the Pink Light every time a cellular memory has been triggered. This is one of the Angels' gifts to humanity. We can all be a part of the greater plan: Heal thyself, heal all. You see, when we are at peace within, we start to grow spiritually and our light becomes brighter and brighter, radiating out into the world and creating waves of positive healing energy. Imagine how powerful that healing light could be if we all stood together shining brightly with the light of Unconditional Love. We could change the world!

The Magenta Pink Light to Heal the Cellular Memory

THIS HEALING EXERCISE IS GENTLE, YET POWERFUL. IT HAS HELPED me and many of my clients, who say after using this beautiful gift that they have gained a new sense of peace and harmony within. Are you ready to accept this wonderful gift and are you ready to love and help yourself? If you have doubts, loving oneself is not selfish, it is self-preservation. Preserve yourself, and doing so you preserve all.

It is now time to heal your subconscious memory.

Sit quietly in a warm room and make yourself comfortable. First and foremost, fill your heart with love. Now reassure yourself you did everything from your heart with the best of intentions at that God given moment in time. When your intentions are pure and actions heart-centered, the moment is always perfect, regardless of the outcome or the way you interpret the event or situation, or how others feel about it. Still your mind, know that you are safe and divinely loved.

Close your eyes, take a few deep breaths and imagine a beautiful bright magenta pink healing light sitting in the palm of your hands. The pink light is an energy of unconditional love and positive healing. This is a gift from our Angelic Friends to heal your cellular memory. Close your eyes. Place your hands over your heart center. Imagine the beautiful bright pink healing light gently swirling out from your hands, and permeating every cell of your being; soothing, loving, forgiving, and healing as it flows. When it reaches the cellular memory of inadequacy, pain, fear, or any other negative emotions, it gently peels a layer back, transforms it into light, and releases it from your energy field.

With each passing layer feelings of positivity deepen. The more you use the magenta pink light the quicker you get to the core of trauma, healing and releasing the negative cellular memory once and for all leaving you with feelings of peace, calm, joy, happiness, forgiveness and love for self and all.

If you are in a public place when a cellular memory has been triggered. Place your hand on your arm or leg and think of the pink light. The above intention has been set and the same outcome will ensue. You will feel it in a gentle way. The Angels will be mindful of the environment you are in. The pink light will be with you for as long as you need it. If you find yourself not using this wonderful gift, ask yourself: *why am I sabotaging my healing process?* Your answer may be: *I don't think I'm worthy*, or, *will this really work for me?* You must understand this is another way that the cellular memory of inadequacy presents itself. Remember, the Angels would not have passed this gift along if they believed we did not deserve it. You have not come across this healing tool by chance. Divine guidance is a beautiful thing.

The Pink Balloon

THE ANGELS GAVE US THE PINK BALLOON TO BREAK NEGATIVE OR sabotaging thoughts. Close your eyes, take three deep breaths and imagine a bright pink balloon with an iridescent blue sheen. These beautiful energetic balloons are limitless, as you release one there is always another one waiting by your side for whenever you need it. This perfect balloon is filled with the purest golden and silver light energy and is able to transmute negativity. When you find yourself in a cycle of negative thought, or when you are internally picking at and criticizing yourself and your life, stop and ask: *why am I doing this?* Are you punishing yourself for something you could have done better, are you feeling guilty, or are you just nitpicking? Whatever the reason is, it is time to let it go and break the continuous negative cycle that does not serve you or anyone else. Remember thoughts create energy.

Imagine your thoughts either like a stream of words or a grey mist gently flowing from your mind or your heart center and floating into your pink balloon. Once they are all inside, release your pink balloon to the Angels. When your pink balloon bursts, your troubled thoughts will have been transformed into positive energy and your Angelic Friends will disperse this throughout the universe. As an added bonus, you will be showered with a golden healing light thus helping you in your quest to create more positive thoughts.

Protecting the Energy Field from Unwanted Energetic Clutter

Many highly sensitive souls, empaths, carry a deep sense of knowing without fully understanding why. They can pick up on and feel other people's sorrows and pain either emotional or physical. They also may react to others thoughts and opinions, which is not always a good thing. When perceiving another's thoughts, especially if those thoughts are personal, empaths can immediately go on the defensive and become what I call an empathic reactor. These interactions always end poorly. When the empath reacts to the thoughts and opinions of others, arguments may arise. The empath can verbally call the other person out even though that person has not verbalized anything. Reacting to another's thoughts can make the empath look a little crazy. I was taught by the Angels to become an emphatic observer. This can take practice. When I first fully awakened, I was given many lessons in non-reaction.

The first lesson I received was while walking up the stairs to join a group of friends at our local Mums and Toddlers group being held at our community church. While ascending the steps, I heard my guide's voice say, "Tracey, you will hear the ladies talking about you and laughing. We want you to know nothing negative has been said about you." I reached the top of the stairs and started to walk around the corner to where the kitchen was situated when I heard a roar of laughter after one of the women mentioned my name. I froze in my tracks. It took me a moment to gather myself as I proceeded to enter the small space that was packed full of ladies, some of which I knew and many I did not. As my presence was seen, a deathly silence consumed the small kitchenette. Only the chatter and the delightful laughter of the children faintly in the background could be heard.

I gazed around at the startled faces and stated "don't worry, I know you didn't bad mouth me. The Angels gave me the heads up!" There was a huge sigh of relief and once again laughter filled the air. They began explaining to me that they had just been comparing the many messages I had delivered to them from their deceased loved ones. Afterwards I asked my guides why they gave me the heads up.

Their reply was quite profound, "Tracey, your intuition will heighten to such a degree that you will feel and sense and sometimes know in-depth conversations that others have spoken about you, whether positive, negative, or indifferent. You must learn to be non-reactive, otherwise you won't be able to do your work. Always know that people will form their own opinions of you and that's okay. Everyone's entitled to their own opinions, likes, and dislikes. These are not necessarily truths. You hold the truth in your own heart. Do not react to another's beliefs. Walk tall, stay neutral, and become the empathic observer. In doing so you will gain great insight."

Have you ever sensed someone's dislike or disapproval of you?

For example, you have been invited to one of your friend's social gatherings. While you are being introduced to a small group of their acquaintances, you instantly sense one of them dislikes you. Your thoughts start to go on the defense, wondering why and thinking: *It is not fair, they do not even know me.* This feeling can affect you so much that you start to react, bringing your mood down, you may possibly begin to give them dirty looks, and before you know it you feel like archenemies. If this continues, everyone becomes uncomfortable and the happy occasion has been sullied. The key to becoming an empathic observer is to be non-reactive to negative thoughts and opinions.

On sensing the judgement or dislike of another, immediately reassure yourself it does not matter, this is only their opinion. You may have even inadvertently triggered a raw nerve within them, or a cellular memory, or insecurity. This is not yours to heal, it is theirs. You know the truth about yourself in your own loving heart. To deal with this situation, warmly smile at them and chat to others in the group. When you learn to become an empathic observer, despite the negative feelings you may feel directed at you, you can deal with the majority of negative thoughts and opinions in any situation.

Transference

EMOTIONAL AND PHYSICAL ENERGY TRANSFERENCE OCCURS WHEN energy is exchanged. Empaths are not always conscious of this or even know they are empathic. Imagine this: you are looking forward to meeting a friend for dinner to cheer her up. On arrival, she hugs you and sits down. Shortly after you begin to feel sad and anxious. You do not understand what has happened as you felt fine before. It may very well be that this sudden emotional pain does not belong to you, it belongs to your friend. Your friend might have started to feel much better, even though she may not understand why, either. Yet, you are left with a deep sense of sadness.

When entering the restaurant your energy field was clear and bright. On an energetic level, your friend's energy field was a little cloudy with worry and sadness. When you embraced and sat down close to one another, you generously and unwittingly gave your friend some sparkly light to help elevate her mood and in return shouldered some of your friend's cloudy energy.

In an example of physical transference, imagine a woman named Julie. Julie's colleague was suffering from a painful knee injury. They had been working closely together on an urgent project. Within a couple of hours Julie's knee began to ache. Julie is quite sensitive and was slightly aware she had picked up on her colleague's pain. She had also sensed what was needed for her colleague to feel better. This energy exchange would immediately help Julie's colleague, even if the colleague was unaware of the transference or how to clear the discomfort from her own knee.

These types of energy transference can stay in your energy field for quite some time. Both may leave the empath feeling physically and energetically fatigued. The more empathic you are, the more you tend to collect the energy of others, which can even occur while standing in line at the grocery store. During transference, many feelings may wash over you, such as sadness, lack of motivation, and heaviness. You are probably not even aware of why you feel this way, and can often tend to go into hibernation-mode in a subconscious effort to clear stagnant energy.

Being sensitive to others is not a bad thing. You are an energy healer, helping others in any way you can, whether you are conscious of it or not. The key is to protect your energy field by using the self-protection and clearing method and not become a metaphorical martyr to the idea that you must suffer when others are suffering. Protecting yourself will not stop you from helping others, quite the contrary, you will be able to help many more. When energetically sensing or feeling another's troubles, you can send them positive healing energy without taking their pains into your energy frequency.

To do this, fill your heart with love. See the person you are wanting to help wrapped in an abundance of golden light that is filled with unconditional love and positive healing energy. Imagine them happy, healthy, and in a physical and emotional state where everything that plagues them is resolved for the highest good of their soul. If you feel you might be invading their energetic privacy, do not worry, their higher-soul-self will use or disregard what you have sent for their greatest good.

Self-Protection and Clearing

BEFORE WE START CONSCIOUSLY OPENING UP TO DIFFERENT ENERGY frequencies, we must learn to protect our own energy fields and living spaces. I cannot emphasize enough the importance of protection. It will make your spiritual journey a lot easier. At the same time, do not be frightened. Lower vibrational energies can only feed off of fear if you allow them. Caring for your own personal energy field is similar to caring for your personal hygiene. Nothing at all to be afraid of, but there are consequences when you do not practice self-protection and energy clearing.

Many years ago, numerous lightworkers became somewhat careless with their energy fields due to the new philosophy of "like attracts like". This idea became a presumption that lightworkers were above attracting any negative energies to themselves. While I understand the concept of "like attracts like", when it comes to protecting your energy field, chances should not be taken, especially regarding those who work in the area of energy clearing. This new belief did not ring entirely true to me. While pondering upon this, I had a vision of a moth being attracted to the light and I asked my guides their thoughts. They told me that until we have pure thoughts every second of every day, we would still attract different energy frequencies. Essentially, no adult person on this earthly plane of duality is one-hundred percent pure in all things. This is not a condemnation, just a reality.

While working to help another soul clear their energy field, where do you think that energy came from? If lightworkers only attracted light and good, how would they encounter those grayer energies that they intend to transmute into positivity and light? This is the method of protection that I have used and taught for over twenty-five years.

The Golden White Egg (Sanctuary)

EVERY MORNING, IDEALLY BEFORE GETTING OUT OF BED, CLOSE your eyes and visualize a beautiful large white egg with golden flecks. At the front of the egg, in the middle, is a two-way zipper, two feet from the top and two feet from the bottom of the egg. Inside the egg, the energy is one of unconditional love, peace, joy, strength, and everything positive that you may need. The egg is spacious and roomy inside so you will not feel confined in any way. Unzip the zipper and step into your egg sanctuary. Zip it up internally. You are now safely tucked away in your energetic shield and this is how it works. From inside out the egg walls are permeable so you are able to send loving and healing light to anyone, any situation, space or place on this planet or beyond. From outside, nothing can penetrate your egg except the purest form of God's light, leaving your energy field totally intact and crystal-clear. Your egg will always be filled with this pure energy. If anyone sends you love or any other positivity, you will still receive it. It will be stored in your beautiful chalice of pure divine light that is situated over your crown chakra. Your Angelic Friends will take care of this topping your egg up accordingly. In addition, if you find yourself having to go in areas that are energetically uncomfortable for you, imagine a beautiful silver and gold shield sitting over your heart center and acting as a buffer so you do not experience the energy of others so intensely.

Protecting Your Soul While You Sleep:
The Golden Cross

IN MY OWN EXPERIENCE, SIMILAR TO THAT OF OTHERS, I HAVE found many empathic souls tend to leave their bodies while they sleep. They work in different realms with the goal of rescuing lost souls and guiding them to the light. This endeavor is important, although some souls are not aware of their nightly work. Others may have a recollection of their task due to an uncomfortable experience while in another realm. At times light workers in all their innocence can wander into realms they should not be in or are unprepared for. When this happens, a person may wake with a jolt and feelings similar to having a bad dream, which can be frightening. My first conscious experience of this was quite scary, to say the least. It had been a long day and after getting the kids to bed, Vic and I thought it would be a good idea to have an early night. As soon as my head hit the pillow I fell into a deep slumber. I awakened in the early hours with my heart thumping and fear pulsating throughout my being. I was so frightened that it took me a while to calm myself. I had a full recollection of what I know to be a psychic attack.

While sleeping, my soul had left my body and I was happily bobbing along doing my work on the astral plane and helping lost souls transition to the light of love, when from afar, I heard a call for help. I knew this was not my area to work in and my intuition said: *stay away.* The call persisted and I found myself conflicted. How could I ignore someone in distress? It went against my nature. Against my better judgment, I started to leave my familiar zone of work and tentatively headed over to the area where the voice came from. As soon as I reached the space where the voice originated, I saw a middle-aged woman with a strange look in her eye. She was sitting in a rocking chair in the middle of a porch. She began gesturing to me to go inside the house. Once again, my heart and soul sensed this was a bad idea. I knew I should not be there. Yet, she was so convincing. Before I knew it, I was inside a room in this strange house. The door slammed shut behind me. I felt trapped. That is when a vortex of dark energy encircled me and wispy grey looking hands began swiping at me and energetically slapping my entire being. The woman's wicked cackle rang in my ears and I knew I had fallen for this trickery once before. I thought: oh no, not again! I closed my eyes and called on the Angels to help me. I was instantly thrust back into my body and woke with a strong sense of fear. I was so irritated with myself for falling for this nonsense.

There are a few reasons why I had this experience. The first reason was to help me formulate a tool to help protect myself and others, which I now call the Golden Cross. Another reason this happened, and why it can happen and has happened to others, is because I, like others, had reached a point where I became a threat to the darkness. My spirit guides informed me that when the light within us grows to such an extent we may attract a grayer energy that intends to knock us off of our mission of light. As I have mentioned before, some hold the belief that light only attracts light. We would not accomplish all of the things we are here to do if within our lives we only ever were exposed to pure light. We might as well never incarnate or leave the light of God's love if that was the case. We are here to bring light into darkness. This leads into the third reason, which was to give me the ability to instantly recognize dark energy masquerading as something it is not. My guides said I learned a lesson in discernment. I silently thanked the dark being for unintentionally giving me these gifts of wisdom, knowing I would never succumb to these tricks again. I no longer had any cause for concern, I only wandered into territory beyond my capability. Perhaps in this situation I decided to have this lesson so I would attain this knowledge. My indecisiveness could have been a decision my higher self needed to make in that instant depending on if I was strong enough to deal with this dark frequency. Or perhaps I did not understand the lesson the first time and I needed to re-experience it to gain wisdom. From whichever perspective, this was a profound lesson.

To avoid having these types of experiences, I came up with a simple, yet powerful tool for protection: the Golden Cross. Before going to sleep at night imagine a beautiful golden light straight down the center of your chakras and another crossing over your heart. The two lines form a cross over the heart center. This is a powerhouse of protection over your soul. The intention is that this protective cross will stop you wandering in realms you should not be in and it has worked perfectly for me for over twenty-five years.

Cleansing Your Physical Living Space

ONCE A MONTH I ENERGETICALLY CLEAR MY HOME AND OFFICE. Beginning in the main bedroom, I prepare the space by opening the windows. I then say a silent prayer and ask my Angelic Friends to assist me in cleansing the area. I visualize that I am holding a beautiful duster formed of golden light specifically created to clear stagnant energy. I start in a corner of the room and use a sweeping motion in every nook and cranny, including the closet. I then visualize sending the grey energy out of the window and ask my Angelic Friends to transform the negative energy into positivity and light, and disperse it throughout the universe. This process is repeated from room to room. When I reach the main living space, I open the back door and the front sending any energy out to be transformed. After this is done, I light my sacred sage smudge stick or palo santo and use the smoke to bless each corner of every room using my hand to form a cross. I also whisper words of protection, love, and blessings for all who reside or walk in this sacred space.

White sage smudge sticks are bound together with twine and palo santo is a piece of wood. Both have been used in sacred ceremonies for thousands of years to heal and cleanse the energy field, spaces and places. This ancient technique is commonly used among indigenous people. Native Americans burn sage to clear and drive out negative energies to help a person or space heal. Also, sage is used to create a sacred space where negative energy cannot enter.

Another tool I like to use to clear my physical space is copal resin. One day, a small copal resin heart spilled out from a small bag as I was preparing to burn the resin. It was bigger than the other pieces and I was excited to receive this little gift. Copal resin is formed when the tree is cut and a thick opaque liquid seeps out. When dry it becomes a pale golden yellow. Revered by the indigenous cultures of the Central and South Americas, it is sacred and has been used in ceremonies since ancient times. Spiritual Healers often burn the resin by lighting a small piece of charcoal on fire. Once hot, the resin is placed on top of the charcoal and as it burns it releases aromatic oils through the smoke. A light citrus fragrance fills the air. Copal resin is used for protection, purification, and clearing the mind from negative thoughts.

When I decided to burn the little heart resin, my guides asked me to take a picture. I did and a little fire heart appeared after lighting the charcoal. I then placed the resin on the charcoal. My guides said: "Feel the energy of the little fire heart of purification. Let it help you cleanse, heal, and release all of your troubles. Place the energies of worry, frustration, irritation, fear, and all that does not serve you well. Focus that into the heart of the copal resin cloud. May you gain clarity, clear thoughts, protection, and purification from all forms of negativity. Remember you are loved unconditionally."

Releasing Lost Souls

FIRST AND FOREMOST, REMEMBER NOTHING FROM THE SPIRIT WORLD can harm you unless you believe it can. If you sense a spirit that may be lost, keep your thoughts loving and positive. In doing so, your energy acts like a beacon of light and is able to assist the lost souls' journey back to the light of God's loving embrace. When sensing lost souls, take a few moments to quieten your mind. Fill your heart with love. Be objective and nonreactive with what energy you may or may not sense emanating from the discarnate soul. Ask your guides and the Angels of Transition to assist you. Be open to listening to or sensing the lost soul's story, sometimes they may want their story to be heard and acknowledged before they can move on. Gently reassure them that when they leave this realm and go to the light all will be forgiven. If you feel it is necessary, encourage the soul to forgive themselves. Reassure them they will not be subjected to the wrath of God, which does not exist. They will be bathed in the light of Unconditional Love.

When you sense they are ready to leave, take a moment to visualize a vertical beam of golden white light filled with the energy of unconditional love, forgiveness, peace, and joy. Ask the Angels of Transition to bring a loved one into the light to greet them. You must be specific and ask for a "loved one" rather than a particular family member just in case they did not have a good relationship with them. Reassure the lost soul that once they step into this magnificent light, they will have a wonderful reunion with their loved one, who will hold them in the most loving embrace and then guide them to the realm or dimension they belong in. Once there they will be on the receiving end of the most joyous celebration of love and reconnection with their loved ones, guides and Angels.

The Energetic Recycling Can

It is okay to experience anger. It is okay to feel frustration. It is okay to be irritated from time to time. Allow yourself a moment to process these feelings in order to identify where they are coming from and what has triggered them. If you cannot make sense of why you feel like this, it may be a cellular memory that has been irritated. Before you use the Pink Light to heal the cellular memory, take a moment to release these feelings by using the energetic recycling can, another gift from the Angels.

The energetic recycling can is here for you to get rid of all of the anger and frustration you may be carrying. Imagine a small recycling bin with two openings. The opening at the top of the bin has "incoming" written in dark green lettering and the bottom of the bin has "outgoing" written with an iridescent silver sheen. Inside the recycling can is the very essence of pure light, specifically placed in your receptacle to help heal any thought that does not serve you or anyone else for their highest good. Transmuting negative energy into positive energy. When your negative thoughts and anger towards others or yourself overwhelms you, set yourself free by releasing these undesirable thoughts. Take a deep breath in through your nose, hold for a moment, and on the exhale imagine your words of frustration and anger leaving your mouth in the form of a grey mist floating down towards the incoming compartment of your trash can. Within an instant, your thoughts have been recycled through the pure light into positive healing energy, which rises out of the outgoing compartment in the form of a fountain filled with all of the colors of a rainbow, now imagine you are being bathed in this blessed light. Each color represents a positive energy being given back to you. Gentle baby blue materializes to calm you; yellow to bring you joy; green to heal you; red for balance and strength; orange to revitalize every cell of your being; and white and gold for unconditional love. Let them wash over you with a soothing wave of love, calm, and peace.

Cleansing and Healing Your Chakras

MAKE YOURSELF COMFORTABLE. TAKE THREE DEEP BREATHS. AS you breathe in, say to yourself *relax*. As you breathe out *release*. Knowing all of your troubles and woes have been transformed into bright lights of positive energy, continue with your breath.

You are now feeling totally and utterly relaxed, safe, and comfortable in the knowledge that you are being held in the light of Divine Love. You now see yourself walking in the most beautiful garden. The sweet floral aroma from the recently bloomed flowers is enchanting. You take a deep breath in, all the while feeling deep gratitude for Mother Nature's gifts. As you saunter, taking in the delightful variety of blossoms in their splendid glory, you notice a magical waterfall of many colors, each color of water is playing a melody of love for you, beckoning you over to bathe and refresh your being in the healing waters of the fall.

You now find yourself basking in the beautiful colors which are permeating every cell of your being, gently loving, soothing, and cleansing you. The water starts to move through your energy centers: first the Crown Chakra, which is located at the top of your head, then your Third-Eye chakra, now your Throat Chakra, gently moving to your Heart Chakra, continuing down through your Solar Plexus Chakra which is located just below the Heart, then the Naval Chakra, and lastly the Root Chakra which is located at the base of your spine. Enjoy the soothing, cleansing energy swirling through your chakra centers removing any unwanted blocks. Now look above you.

The waterfall has changed color to a golden–silver light.

The golden-silver light now begins to flow towards you, gently soothing and moving through every cell of your being, filling you with the light of Unconditional Love. Take a moment to enjoy this feeling. Now step out of the light and sit yourself down on the beautiful bench you see before you with your feet firmly planted on the ground. Your body begins to feel at one with your mind and soul. It is now time to come back into awareness. You have been on a wonderful healing journey, one which you will always cherish. Start to wiggle your fingers and toes, stretch your arms, take a few relaxing breaths, and when you are ready, open your eyes. Welcome back.

Prayer to Assist the World During Challenging Times

THE ANGELS HAVE ASKED US TO JOIN TOGETHER TO RADIATE A wave of light out into the world. They say it will make a huge difference to all during challenging times. Hold the intention that this light of positive healing energy will eradicate any issue that is not for the greatest good of all and replace it with the vibration of love and wellbeing. It only takes a couple of minutes and you can join in this prayer anytime. Close your eyes and calm your mind. Take three deep breaths knowing that you are safe and divinely loved. Imagine you are holding the world in the palm of your hands. Now visualize the light of Unconditional Love and positive healing energy permeating every cell of your being, calming and soothing. Your heart is now filled with so much love it begins to overflow, pouring out in the form of white light with an iridescent golden sheen surrounding the world and all who reside here. The Angels thank you for your beautiful light. It will be magnified tenfold and will be used to assist all. Their wish is that you have good health, a peaceful heart, happiness, and an abundance of love.

The Violet Flame

YOU CAN INVOKE THE VIOLET FLAME TO HEAL AND CLEANSE negativity from yourself, others or the planet. Make yourself comfortable; close your eyes; take three deep breaths. As you breathe in, say to yourself, *relax*, as you breathe out, *release*, continue to focus on your breath. You are now feeling totally and utterly relaxed, safe, and comfortable in the knowledge that you are being held in divine light with the keepers of the Violet Flame, Kwan Yin to your left and Saint Germain to your right. Imagine the Violet Flame in your mind's eye: a fire with colors of dark indigo, sparkling purple, and violet with swirls of rose pink gently flowing upward towards the tip of the flame. Now see yourself surrounded by this beautiful, sacred light. The flames rise around you, pulsating and permeating every cell of your being, releasing and transmuting all negativity, and leaving you feeling cleansed and whole. You may now send the light of the Violet Flame to any one, anything, any space on the planet, or beyond. When complete, imagine your whole being wrapped in silver and gold light. The feeling of being loved unconditionally fills your heart, mind and soul. The Ascended Masters bow to you and thank you for your service to the world. With deep gratitude for their loving assistance, bow and thank them. It is now time to come back into awareness. You have been on a wonderful mission of light. Wiggle your fingers and toes, stretch your arms, take a few relaxing breaths, and when you are ready to, open your eyes. Welcome back.

The Akashic Records

THE HALL OF KNOWLEDGE IS A UNIVERSAL MEMORY BANK CREATED at the inception of time. It records every thought, action, feeling, and intention from all souls in past, present, and future lifetimes. Occasionally, it is beneficial to access this Divine Wisdom to gain clarity and insight on certain issues that may be restricting your spiritual growth, thus aiding your journey toward a more enlightened state of being. Many people use meditation as a tool to access this wisdom from the Akashic Records.

Please make yourself comfortable. We are now going on a journey to access the Akashic Records. You may know this as the Hall of Knowledge, where all records of who you are and who you have ever been are kept. You will be shown only the information that will be beneficial and pertinent to your present life, all the while knowing you are perfectly safe and held in the Golden Light of Unconditional Love. Take some deep breaths. As you breathe in, relax. As you breathe out, release all the tension and frustrations you may be holding. Continue with your breath. As you breathe, visualize a golden white light moving down through the top of your head and permeating every cell of your being. Radiant waves of Divine Love, move slowly and smoothly through you. As the light of love moves throughout your body, you feel total oneness with all that is and all that will be.

You are now standing before the closed entrance to the great Hall of Knowledge. This door is a magnificent arched masterpiece with many carvings depicting the life forms of every being from every realm that ever existed. Take a moment to study this awe-inspiring door. Trace your fingers over the elaborate carvings. Inhale the soothing aroma of ancient sandalwood. Know that beyond the door is absolute knowledge where judgement does not exist. You are seen as love no matter who you are or who you have been. Leave all fear behind. Now gently push the doors. As the doors open inwardly, the custodian of the Akashic Records steps forward to greet you. He is a wise elder with eyes like twinkling diamonds, filled with love and compassion for you. His grey hair and well-groomed beard glistens with a sparkling silver sheen. No words need to be exchanged; he already knows what you seek. He now leads you down a softly illuminated corridor to a small room. You enter and are instantly drawn to a bright light situated in the center of the room. The light beckons you to sit at the desk and chair beneath it. Take a moment to bask in this soothing, loving golden light. As you begin to look around the room, you see that you are surrounded by many books with specific knowledge of your souls' very existence. You are filled with a sense of excitement as you see your custodian outstretch his arm and instantly one of the books floats with ease to his hand. He smiles kindly at you as he gently places the book before you. He quietly leaves the room.

You may now open the book to a page of your choice. There will be one or more messages for you. Take a moment to feel, sense, and digest the meaning of your message. Feel the true essence of the information in your heart. Know that what you have received is a wonderful gift for you to cherish. Take your time. When you feel ready, close the book.

Now leave the room and step into the corridor. In the corridor, the custodian greets you and escorts you back to the magnificent arched doorway. As you gaze into the custodian's twinkling eyes you know he is wishing you well on your present journey. You may now offer him a gift to aid the world. This gift can be your love, it can be a pledge to help others, whatever comes to you from your heart will be perfect.

It is now time to walk through the door. As you do so, you carry a sense of peace and calm and feelings of great love for yourself and all life. Know that this feeling will always be with you. It is now time to come back into awareness. You have been on a wonderful journey and now you are going to come back to the present. Imagine yourself sitting on a comfortable wooden bench with your feet firmly planted on the ground beneath you. The slight aroma of fresh flowers permeates the air. Feelings of joy, and love fill your mind, heart, and soul. Start to wiggle your fingers and toes. Stretch your arms and take a few relaxing breaths and, when you are ready, open your eyes; Welcome back.

The Cosmic Chakra

DURING GLOBAL TIMES OF CHANGE AND TRANSFORMATION, OUR bodies can become very sensitive to the fluctuating energy frequencies of Mother Earth, often leading to confusion and doubt. Many practices aid in the grounding of one's energy, such as yoga, meditation, prayer, and exercise, but it is possible to become too grounded, which can cause us to feel energetically restricted. As the earth goes through its recalibration, we must also be able to flow with her changes and rebalance ourselves in her new energy. Over the years, I noticed some empathic souls have been struggling to adapt to these unseen energy changes. The Angels offered a solution to this impasse and gifted us with a vibrational download: "The Cosmic Chakra". Participating in this meditation just once will aid in keeping your energy grounded while also enabling you to gently flow with the fluctuations of the earth's vibration that we will all be experiencing for quite a few years. The Cosmic Chakra is filled with Unconditional Love and brings the highest good to all life.

Make yourself comfortable. Take three deep breaths. As you breathe in, think silently to yourself: *relax*. As you breathe out, think silently to yourself: *release*. Know that all your troubles and woes will be transformed into bright lights of positive energy with each passing breath. Continue to focus on your breath. You are now feeling totally and utterly relaxed, safe, and comfortable in the knowledge that you are being held in the Light of Divine Love. Now see before you a vertical tunnel of golden light radiating outward. In the light, you can see tiny sparkling silver orbs welcoming you, offering to cleanse and heal every cell of your being.

You feel drawn to the light. The warmth that emanates from the light fills you with a sense of great love and peace. Step into the tunnel of light, feel the iridescent gold and silver healing energy releasing all that does not serve you well. Feelings of rejuvenation and a sense of being reborn now fill all your senses. Take a few moments to enjoy this beautiful feeling. The channel of golden light begins to slowly and gently move away from you. This feeling of well-being stays with you, and you now feel ready to have your connection with the Cosmic Chakra.

The Cosmic Chakra is situated three feet above the top of your head. You see its colors of vibrant violet dancing, swirling, and merging with the brightest blue-turquoise you could ever imagine, while radiating and pulsating waves of celestial light and filling space and time with divine Unconditional Love.

Take a moment to gaze at the Cosmic Chakra and all its splendor. Now bring your attention to your Heart Chakra. Colors of gentle green and rose pink accompany feelings of comfort and great love for yourself and all life. Take a moment to enjoy this wonderful feeling.

You now begin to sense a beautiful ruby-red light starting to swirl in the middle of the green and rose pink. This ruby-red light becomes stronger and stronger, brighter and brighter. It starts to move downward through your Solar Plexus Chakra, and now your Naval Chakra, and steadily it moves down through the Base Chakra. The ruby-red light continues down towards a beautiful crystalline pyramid located at the center of Mother Earth. Once there, the bright ruby red light enters the crystal pyramid. As it does, an explosion of rainbows fill the pyramid and extend outwards and upwards in all directions, filling the earth with beautiful healing rainbow light. Take a moment to enjoy this marvelous sight.

When you are ready, bring your focus back to your Heart Chakra. Focus on the colors of green, rose pink and the bright ruby-red light. Now you see a beautiful bright blue-turquoise light begin to flow and to connect to the ruby-red light. As it does, the blue-turquoise and ruby-red light swirl together as one, securing the connection between the ruby-red light and the beautiful bright blue-turquoise light, which gently starts to move upwards towards the throat chakra. It then moves towards the Third Eye Chakra. It continues up and through your Crown Chakra, reaching the Cosmic Chakra, where it connects, merging and swirling with a vibrant violet and a bright blue-turquoise. Enjoy this feeling of connection and completion. Feel joy in every cell of your being. Know that you will be free to move without limitation during all vibrational energy changes, while at the same time remaining safely grounded. It is now time to come back into the present moment.

Imagine your body to be a beautiful warm cozy coat. As you slip into this wonderful coat called your body, know that it will cherish and look after you in the best way that it can. Start to wiggle your fingers and toes, take a few breaths, stretch, and when you feel ready, open your eyes.

Little Manifestations

For many years, my guides have communicated with me by pointing out formations that they have manifested as symbols for the messages they want to convey. Since I received the Rainbow Heart Light energy, the frequency of these manifestations has intensified. The Angels have been directing my attention and awareness to all of the images that have manifested around me and now encourage me to take pictures. Whenever I am nudged by my guides and Angelic Friends, I do take a picture. While reviewing the pictures, my guides share messages to comfort or inspire me, or to help comfort and inspire others. My photo library is now full of reminders of their love and the love from Creator God. These images, as well as many others, have been made available for viewing in color on my website: www.theRainbowHeartLight.com.

The Rainbow Angel

On a cold winter day more than twenty years ago, Oliver, who was only a little boy at the time, and I were out shopping at our local open-air market when I noticed an amazing stall filled with the most vibrant crystals I had ever seen. We went over to investigate. I was drawn to this beautiful crystal ball and as I picked it up, it lit up with the image of an Angel with rainbow wings. The cost was £22 GBP. I did not have a spare penny at the time. I thought to myself: I would love to buy it, if only I had the money. All of a sudden, the lady selling the crystals looked me in the eye and said, "take it home. You can pay via installments over the next few weeks. It wants to go home with you." The kind and generous woman introduced herself as Carol.

Carol, whom we affectionately call Crystal Carol, did not even ask me for my phone number or address. She had absolute trust in her own strong intuition, knowing I would be true to my word and pay her for the crystal ball. This was also the start of a lifelong friendship. The love she has for the mineral world is unsurpassed, making her a true custodian of our crystal friends. I had treasured this piece for twenty-two years when I heard a message from the Angels: *Take a picture of the Rainbow Angel. It's time to share.*

May the Rainbow Angel bless you and touch your heart with love, so that you may express the trust, love, kindness, and generosity within you, as Carol did, and open yourself up to true friendship.

The Rebirth of a New Consciousness

THIS LITTLE ANGEL WITH HER BEATING HEART MANIFESTED OVER one of my energy paintings called, "The Rebirth of a New Consciousness". It was early morning and I had gone into my office to prepare for the arrival of my first client of the day. I smiled to myself and thanked the Angels for this beautiful blessing. My client arrived and the Angels revealed that she had recently lost her best friend. This little Angel appeared as a blessing for my client and for all to remind us that our loved ones can return to us from beyond the veil on the wings of love to lift and help us through our grief.

"The Rebirth of a New Conscious" depicts the energy of a new, more loving way of being. This way of being would create and bring forth a more loving and harmonious world, with compassion, hope, and kindness as the motivating forces of the shared human experience. As we all work through our own trials, tribulations, and grief in a positive way, remember that we are all working towards this new way of being to bring forth this world together with compassion in our hearts.

The message for the world from my guides after channeling this painting: *You are experiencing a recalibration of your mind, body, and soul! The process has been accelerated and intensified over the last few months. This reconstruction has been triggered by waves of light energy flowing through and around each of you and the Earth! She, too, is recalibrating, raising her frequencies. This huge rebirth is touching all and bringing about a new consciousness. During this time, you may experience temporary feelings of sadness, uncertainty, frustration, then moments of intense joy! You might become more sensitive to chemicals, nudging you to eat a nontoxic diet with less animal protein, if any at all. You also may be experiencing physical aches and pains for no apparent reason. Feeling the need to hibernate, thus, giving yourself time to reflect on many outdated patterns. It might feel negative at times but in all truth, it is a most wonderful new way of being and a blessing for all. The key is to keep quiet and non-reactive, even if your challenges are extreme. Surround yourself with the most beautiful bright violet blue light and imagine a silver shield placed over your heart center. This will help you move through this transition with ease and grace.*

Angel Healing of Light
– January 2018

MY FAMILY AND I HAD JUST SOLD OUR HOME AND WERE IN THE process of packing the house up. Lewis had just told me he had joined the army and I was a little off of my game. I was sitting on a stool shredding old documents when the paper shredder got jammed. I grabbed a sharp pocket knife and proceeded to unblock the opening. I still do not know how I did it, but I sliced my finger right down the side of my nail. I felt queasy and nearly fainted, which is out of character for me because I am usually fine at the sight of blood and have a high pain tolerance. The kids patched me up, unblocked the shredder, and carried on loading the moving truck to take our belongings to the rental property we were moving into. Thirty minutes later, I was back on my stool feeling sorry for myself and my throbbing finger, when I heard from the Angels, "Tracey, cheer up and look up". To my surprise! The image of a little Angel healing of light appeared on the ceiling. I felt the wave of love filled light soothe my soul instantly, lifting my spirit and easing the pain in my finger. Even when we feel everything in the moment is going wrong, the Angels are still here, helping to guide us all through difficult times, and reminding us that this too shall pass.

Healing Angel that appeared on the ceiling.

The Inner Heart Rose
– November 2013

I WAS URGED TO GO OUTSIDE TO TAKE A PICTURE OF THE ROSES that had bloomed. A heart appeared inside of a yellow and peach colored rose. My guides gave this message: *Give yourself a hug. Dry your tears, feel the blanket of love draped over your shoulders and remember there is no distance between the energy of love. Your hearts are always connected. When you think of your deceased family member or friend you instantly send them your love. Imagine this love like sparkling, light-filled rose petals of many colors, each color symbolizing a gift to them. This may be happiness, love, joy, peace, or forgiveness, or whatever comes to your mind is fine. The petals emanate from your heart center, moving out in a stream of pure golden-white twinkling light and gently swirling and flowing beyond the veil to your loved one's heart center. Your loved one feels this beautiful gift and simultaneously sends their love right back to you. You are filled with many energetic treasures to aid you on your journey, creating an eternal circle of light.*

The Sacred Rose Heart - June 2016

ON THIS BRIGHT MORNING, I WAS BUSILY SCURRYING AROUND THE house getting ready for work when I heard, "Tracey, a special rose has just come into bloom. Go outside and look."

We had about a dozen rose bushes bordering the path to our front door, so I asked, "which one?"

My guide replied, "you will see."

I stopped what I was doing and popped out of the front door of my home to scan over the roses. My eyes had locked on to the brightest pink heart-shaped rose. I took a moment to feel the love emanating from this beautiful flower then ran back inside to alert the family of this special gift we had received. The Angels told me to capture the image and the love emanating from the rose.

Later that day this message came from our Angelic Friends:

Stay pure of heart and love will reign supreme.

The rose opens its heart while boldly bathing in the bright light of the sun. If the rose did not have absolute trust, we would never see its inner beauty! Do you have the courage to stand open-hearted in the light of Unconditional Love and shine your beautiful heart light into the world? Do not be afraid to be you! Some may not understand, like, or agree with you. That is absolutely fine. They are entitled to their opinion. You know your own truth. You do not have to convince anyone. Stay true to the Wisdom of the Heart and remember you are brave, beautiful, and unique, just like the Sacred Heart Rose.

Pegasus – October 2016

On October 8, 2016, I was in the car, waiting for the traffic lights to change, when I heard the familiar otherworldly voices of my guides say, "Tracey, look up, you will see Pegasus." I quickly took a snap of this amazing formation just before the traffic lights turned green. My guides said: *Pegasus is a symbol of the time of new consciousness, which will bring forth a whole new civilization of heart-centered souls. This mythical being brings a tremendous gift to humanity. Pegasus carries the energy of joy, good health, and prosperity. Humanity is going through a time of change and transformation. Although this may take any number of years, and no matter what challenges humanity goes through, the light will prevail. Pegasus, with his strong wings, rises above any negativity, and so can we.*

Pegasus cloud formation in October, 2016.

The Sword of Truth – December 2016

ARCHANGEL MICHAEL'S SWORD OF TRUTH APPEARED TO ME ON December 2nd, 2016. Their message was: *The Sword of Truth brings forth the spiritual warrior inside each of you. With Unconditional Love in your heart, are you willing to stand up for what you believe is right? Or have you resigned yourself to allowing injustice to unfold in a situation over which you feel you have no control? Archangel Michael is the Angel of Protection. Ask him to surround you with a protective shield of divine light to keep you safe as you stand up for Truth. We can speak the truth, without fear of judgement, in a gentle and non-violent way, when it comes from the wisdom of the heart. Remember to keep out of your mental mind, and listen to your heart when deciding what is the truth and what is not. Your heart is your moral compass. When you struggle to find your voice, focus on bringing the loving light into your heart and radiate it outwards. By acknowledging, feeling, and knowing the truth, your energy speaks for you.*

Archangel Michael's Sword of Truth.

Fluffy Heart Cloud – September 2017

I WAS DRIVING HOME FROM WORK ON SEPTEMBER 11TH, 2017 WHEN I was asked by my guides to look up at the sky. A large fluffy heart cloud appeared before my eyes. I pulled over and captured it on my phone before it began to disperse. My Angelic Friends urged me to write a message: *When there is the suffering of a family member, friend, animal, stranger or place, they need positive energy. The thoughts that first enter your mind are fear, sadness, worry, anger, and helplessness. These are perfectly normal. Acknowledge them and give yourself a little time to empathize and sympathize with the situation. Accept it, knowing you will do everything within your capabilities on a practical level to help. Now give yourself a huge dose of love to bring your heart and mind to equilibrium. You can do this by placing your left hand on your right shoulder and your right hand on your left shoulder. This creates the infinity sign. Imagine all the love being sent to you from every soul that has known and loved you from every different realm. Feel this love in your hands remembering to place your love there, too. Take a moment to feel that eternal loving hug, feel it permeating every cell of your being while soothing, loving, calming, strengthening, and reassuring as it flows. Take a moment to receive this gift of love. Now you are ready to send your blessing.*

Fill your heart with love. Visualize the ones you are concerned for bathed in a golden light of Unconditional Love and positive healing energy. See them happy and healthy. Picture everything resolving for the highest good of their soul and for the good of those around them. This will help them tremendously. They do not have to be aware of the blessing you have sent them. Their soul will use this much needed energy exactly at the right moment in time.

If your thoughts return to fear or worry, stop your thoughts and repeat the blessing. Always remember thoughts create energy. By keeping your thoughts positive through challenging times, you get through them swiftly with ease and grace.

Heart cloud formation in September, 2017.

Water Hearts and Cetaceans

MY DEAR FRIEND, MICHELLE ANDERSON, CO-HOST ON THE Awakening Radio Show, is a lover of humanity, an environmentalist, and an ambassador of peace. A few times a year, she gathers like-minded souls and organizes a private charter on the catamaran out of Dana Point Harbor. This gathering is known as the Divine Dolphin and Whale "Live Your Bliss" Cruise. The intention of this gathering is to send Unconditional Love and healing to every being; bringing peace, harmony and balance to every realm. I look forward to these gatherings. Ever since I was a little girl, I have adored dolphins. These sentient beings are intelligent and playful. They teach us joy through connection and express their love through various sound frequencies, reminding us to voice our love for one another. Dolphins also teach us the importance of community and the true value of the youngest members of our communities, our children. When a dolphin is born, its mother holds her newborn to the surface to take its first breaths. Dolphin mothers keep their babies close to their sides for up to three years. Adult dolphins instinctively protect their children, they encourage us to step into the energy of playfulness and to incorporate laughter back into our lives. Reminding us not to lose connection to our inner child. Observing dolphins is a wonderful way to regain balance and to feel revitalized, especially during turbulent times.

On a cruise held during the summer solstice, 2018, we encountered a large pod of dolphins. The sparkle of the rays of the sun on the ocean showed us an ocean heart light. After raising the vibration and sending love and healing to all life and giving thanks and prayers to the waters of the world, the Angels told me the water would form a heart and I would capture this manifestation on film. They said it was Gaia's way of showing us her love and appreciation for our positive intentions, thoughts, prayers and love. They do make a difference.

Even though this event occurred in the past, you can still join in, if you feel called. All you have to do is fill your heart with loving intentions. Imagine the light of love forming a ray of golden sparkling energy emanating from your heart and beaming out to the center of the Ocean's heart. This will instantly add to the wave of unconditional love and positive healing energy that has been created for the greatest good of all life in every realm and dimension.

The Prosperity Pumpkin and Flying Pigs – October 2018

I HAD WEARILY CLIMBED OUT OF BED, READIED MYSELF FOR WORK, and made my way downstairs in an effort to tidy up the kitchen before leaving the house. I quickly loaded the dishwasher and then noticed Vic's empty coffee cup on the side table. I sighed and walked over to retrieve it. I have never been able to successfully train Vic to do it himself (only kidding). I saw this perfect little pumpkin inside the coffee cup and heard my spirit guides laugh and say: "It's a prosperity pumpkin."

I started to chuckle. It was pumpkin season, after all. I found out later that the pumpkins represent harvest, abundance, and prosperity. While this was a personal message for Vic and his company, and an effort by the Angels to start my morning with some fun and a sense of humor, it was also a message to share with the world. The pumpkin itself is a world and each seed represents an opportunity to create a positive intention which will grow and bring abundance to your life and to the lives of others.

The Angels have a fantastic sense of humor. They often reiterate that laughter is the best medicine. One night, they decided to drive this message home. Friends of ours had asked us to join them for a night at the comedy club in Hermosa Beach. Our night was filled with so much laughter we felt we were going to burst. After we said our goodbyes to our friends and thanked them for a wonderful evening, we hopped in our car. While driving home and listening to music, I was once again urged to look. To my surprise a little pig cloud was in the night sky. I heard my Angels say, "Tracey, pigs really do fly."

Prosperity pumpkin appearing at the bottom of Vic's cup of coffee.

Flying pig cloud formation appearing in the sky after a night out.

Ode to T. O'M by Victoria

IN ONE OF TRACEY'S LIVES, SHE LIVED AS A MAN NAMED TOM. TOM was a romantic, a poet, writer, and dreamer. Upon finding Tom's work, his father, who wanted him to follow a more prestigious line of work, burned Tom's life's work of poems, letters, essays, and stories. Brokenhearted and ashamed, Tom said he would never write again.

As long as I have known Tracey, she has had an intense resistance to sharing herself through the written word. Many of us have asked this from her. She will often say she is "not a writer," that it is not something she was gifted with. The task of writing this alone was painfully arduous for her, which is understandable, considering that sharing oneself in this way creates a permanent vulnerability.

I can speak on behalf of Tracey's family and dearest friends when I say we are proud of her for overcoming her fears and sharing her unique perspective with us. I am glad that by sharing her story the residue cellular memory of Tom is healed and the next chapter of Tracey's story can manifest.

Printed in the United States
by Baker & Taylor Publisher Services